APM
BODY OF KNOWLEDGE

APM
BODY OF KNOWLEDGE

Sixth edition

Association for Project Management

Association for Project Management
Ibis House, Regent Park
Summerleys Road, Princes Risborough
Buckinghamshire
HP27 9LE

© Association for Project Management 2012

Sixth edition 2012
Fifth edition 2006
Fourth edition 2000
Third edition 1996
Second edition 1994
First edition 1992

Paperback: ISBN:978-1-903494-40-0

Hardback: ISBN 978-1-903494-41-7

Ebook: ISBN 978-1-903494-42-4

Typeset in 11/14pt Foundry Sans
Printed and bound by Imprint Digital
Cover design by Fountainhead, Middlesex

Contents

List of figures

Preface

Welcome to the *APM Body of Knowledge 6th Edition*, a crucial document for our profession and an important contribution towards our vision of a world in which all projects succeed.

In describing ourselves as the Association for Project Management, we use the phrase "Project Management" to cover three different but related and overlapping approaches – project management, programme management and portfolio management. Each of these is covered in this edition. Together, they provide a professional approach to managing change, the universal challenge of the modern age.

This document helps us structure our thinking and activities more widely than before to respond to this challenge. It is the product of a collaborative project involving more than 1,000 practitioners, experts and academics from a broad range of sectors and backgrounds. It presents the fundamental structure of project management functions and updates and extends the glossary of terms.

We are fortunate in being able to anchor our discipline in a robust structure and taxonomy which can develop, evolve and progress by using the technology now available to us. Hence we are also providing an online facility that allows you to contribute to the further evolution of thinking and practice in the profession.

This publication is the end of one project but more importantly it is the start of another – the discussion that will continue to develop our knowledge base as we pursue our vision.

Mike Nichols, APM Chairman

Acknowledgements

The development of a body of knowledge is a complex, time-consuming and intellectually stimulating activity. It would not be possible without extensive and diverse contributions from the many people and organisations that make up the project, programme and portfolio community.

It is important that these voluntary contributions are recognised as a way of saying thank you and to demonstrate the community's ownership of the material. This collective ownership is what makes the *APM Body of Knowledge* unique amongst its kind.

Firstly, we recognise the contributors of the reference materials that have enriched the content through the 1000s of hours authoring, re-writing, discussion and debate.

Secondly, we thank the many parties from a wide range of backgrounds, locations and industry sectors who attended review events, focus groups and virtual reviews, approaching these tasks with thoroughness and patience.

Thirdly, we acknowledge the many individuals who have contributed by writing or checking or commenting on draft sections. They have done this as individuals, on behalf of their organisations or in steering groups during 2010 and 2011.

Fourthly, we would also like to acknowledge the many organisations that have permitted or encouraged their staff to contribute as individuals and have provided collected corporate views to the process.

Fifthly, there are the editorial and production teams who have assembled this edition and its supporting website.

We should also acknowledge the diverse collection of end users who will develop the knowledge contained within the *APM Body of Knowledge* and create new and innovative ways of working towards a world in which all projects succeed.

Thank you to all participants and stakeholders in the *APM Body of Knowledge*.

Acknowledgements

A wide variety of experts and practitioners have been involved in the various phases of development of the *APM Body of Knowledge 6th edition*. APM is grateful for the time, effort and expertise they put into the project.

Acaster, Michael
Agapiou, Dr Andrew MAPM
Ajala, Anthony Babatunde
  MAPM
Akrofi, Solomon RPP MAPM
Alba, Joseph F S RPP FAPM
Ali, Dr Mushtaq
Allsworth, Aaron MAPM
Anstey, Richard FAPM
Apsley, Lee MAPM
Assirati, Bob CBE HonFAPM
Atkinson, David FAPM
Baker, Rod RPP FAPM
Balchin, Colin MAPM
Ballard, Peter D
Banerjee, Arnab
Barron, Steve
Barrow, Helen
Bartlett, John FAPM
Bell, Carol RPP FAPM
Belsey, Adrian RPP MAPM
Bennett, Dean
Bilsborough, Jeanette MAPM
Bird, David T MAPM
Bishop, Martin
Bhatt, Rajesh
Blackall, Kate
Blakemore, Peter
Bolton, John RPP MAPM
Bragg, Andrew
Branwhite, Sarah MAPM
Bright, David MAPM
Britton, Jane FAPM
Brown, Amanda
Brown, Michael HonFAPM
Brown, Steve
Browne, Jenn MAPM
Browne, Steve
Brownlee, Ben MAPM
Bryden, John FAPM

Burney-Cumming, Ed MAPM
Burton, David RPP MAPM
Bushell, Tim MAPM
Buttrick, Robert
Bye-Jorgensen, Lucy
Campbell, Peter FAPM
Carpenter, Julian MAPM
Caton, John MAPM
Chapman, John MAPM
Charters, Steve MAPM
Chick, Martin MAPM
Childs, Tiffany
Chita, Pritam
Christie, Edel MAPM
Clarke, Caroline MAPM
Clark, Peter W J MAPM
Clarkson, Dr Ian
Clunas, David MAPM
Collier, Brian MAPM
Collins, Glenn
Connolly, John
Coombes, Brian MAPM
Cornish, John
Coverdale, Stuart MAPM
Cropper, John MAPM
Cummins, Tim
Curtis, Dr Bernard HonFAPM
Curtis, Peter MAPM
Curtis, Neil MAPM
Dalcher, Professor Darren
  HonFAPM
Dale, James
Dallas, Michael MAPM
Daly, John MAPM
Dann, Jill
Darch, Brian
Davis, Alex MAPM
Deary, Peter MAPM
Delo, Dr Andrew FAPM
Devin, Jonathan

Devine, Graham MAPM
Dixon, Miles MAPM
Docherty, Mark
Docker, Dr Thomas MAPM
Don, Ronald Murray
Dooley, Adrian HonFAPM
Dove, Simon MAPM
Duffy, Geraldine RPP MAPM
Duncan, Angus MAPM
Dunning, David MAPM
Edwards, David MAPM
Edwards, Tom MAPM
Egbu, Professor Charles FAPM
Egginton, Dr Bill RPP FAPM
Evans, Eleri MAPM
Ferguson, Alan
Ferguson, Sian
Fielden, Bob MAPM
Fisher, John MAPM
Fletcher, Howard J RPP FAPM
Fowler, Nigel MAPM
Franklin, Melanie MAPM
Franklin, Neil MAPM
Fry, Esther
Garcia, Jose Eduardo Motta
Garrini, Roger RPP MAPM
Gawler, Keith RPP MAPM
Gilbert, Alec
Gilbert, Commander Peter
  RPP MAPM
Gildas, Andre MAPM
Gleich, Rev Nicholas MAPM
Glen, Ewan RPP MAPM
Glynne, Peter FAPM
Godbold, Alistair RPP FAPM
Golding, David MAPM
Goodge, Paul RPP FAPM
Goodman, Elisabeth MAPM
Gordon, John FAPM
Gould, Simon

Gosden, Martin RPP FAPM
Gray, Eur Ing Andrew
Greenan, Alastair FAPM
Griffin, Michael
Grounsell, Evelyn
Halligan, Paul MAPM
Hamilton, James P G MAPM
Hampton, Jacquie MAPM
Hancock, Gill
Hanif, Dr Tahir MAPM
Hardy, Simon
Hargraves, Anthony MAPM
Harries, Sarah MAPM
Harris, Annie MAPM
Harris, Julian MAPM
Harrison, Eur Ing Dr Keith
  MAPM
Harrison, Robin MAPM
Hart, David RPP MAPM
Hartley, Nina MAPM
Hawkins, Peter MAPM
Hayward, Eur Ing Nigel
  RPP MAPM
Hazeldine, Major Donald
  Philip RPP MAPM
Higgins, Michael
Hinks, Hilary RPP MAPM
Heathcote, John MAPM
Herdman, Mike MAPM
Hewins, Terry MAPM
Hillson, Dr David HonFAPM
Hindley, Guy N FAPM
Hobson, Chris FAPM
Hodgkins, Paul FAPM
Holder, Anne MAPM
Horsted, Peter MAPM
Howard, Jon MAPM
Howes, Trevor MAPM
Inge, James MAPM
Jarrett, Elwyn MAPM
Jemmison, Phillip MAPM
Jenkins, Paul RPP MAPM
Jenner, Stephen FAPM
Johns, Nicholas FAPM

Johnson, Bill MAPM
Johnson, Chris RPP MAPM
Johnson, Peter MAPM
Jonas, Val MAPM
Jones, Alan MAPM
Jones, Andrew FAPM
Jones, Geoffrey
Jones, Sion Penrhyn MAPM
Joseph, Howard MAPM
Joshi, Ravi
Josserand, François MAPM
Kane, Dr Kevin RPP MAPM
Kelly, Louise MAPM
Kent, Adrian MAPM
Kimmins, Mike RPP MAPM
Kinsella, Martin
Krolikowski, Andrew MAPM
Laird, John
Lake, John RPP MAPM
Lane, Ken
Langdon, Mark FAPM
Langley, Jo MAPM
Laughlin, John MAPM
Launchbury, Maura MAPM
Laurillard, Mark MAPM
Lawrence, Nick RPP MAPM
Leat, Dave MAPM
Lester, Albert HonFAPM
Lillicrap, David MAPM
Linde, Lizanne
Lock, Dennis FAPM
Lomas, Mark Gowan RPP
  MAPM
Londeix, Bernard MAPM
Long, Carol MAPM
Lord, Pamela
Lowther, Gwynne
Lyons, Tim MAPM
MacDonald,Irene FAPM
MacKinnon, John FAPM
MacNicol, Donnie MAPM
Mapes, Simon
Markham, Nicola MAPM
Martin, Camilla MAPM

Mason, Dr Ian MAPM
Mason, Stephen MAPM
Masters, John MAPM
Mather, James MAPM
McElroy, Bill FAPM
McEwen, Jason MAPM
McGregor, John MAPM
McKinlay, Mary FAPM
McLaughlan, Robert
McPherson, Alan RPP MAPM
Millard, Roy FAPM
Mills, Gillian
Milner, Sean RPP MAPM
Minney, Dr Hugo MAPM
Mitchell, Dr Cliff MAPM
Mitchell, Tony MAPM
Moaby, Mark MAPM
Mooney, Neil RPP MAPM
Morris, Professor Peter
  W G HonFAPM
Mostafa, Hosam FAPM
Murray, Andy MAPM
Murray-Webster, Ruth MAPM
Murton, Mala MAPM
Mystris, Peter
Neve, John
Nevin, Michael MAPM
Newell, Simon MAPM
Nichols, Michael Dane FAPM
Norman, Mark
O'Callaghan, John
O'Brien, Liz MAPM
Oliver, Mark RPP MAPM
Osborne, Alan MAPM
O'Shea, Dr Keith
Parkes, Dr Peter FAPM
Parrett, Stephen MAPM
Parry, Kevin MAPM
Payne, David Anthony
Pellegrinelli, Dr Sergio
Perry, Shushma
Perry, Tony FAPM
Platts, Kenneth MAPM
Powell, David FAPM

Acknowledgements

Preston, Richard HonFAPM
Price, Martin
Pullan, Penny
Purser, Claire MAPM
Purslow, Corin MAPM
Pyne, Adrian RPP MAPM
Rawlins, Mike
Rawson, Matt RPP MAPM
Rayner, Paul HonFAPM
Reeder, Morag MAPM
Reeson, Mark FAPM
Reid, Allan FAPM
Rigby, Christine MAPM
Rivera, Ivan
Rivkin, Dr Steve FAPM
Robinson, Ann
Roden, Eileen J MAPM
Rodriguez, Marta Moreira
  MAPM
Royden, Jane MAPM
Rush, Brian MAPM
Ryan, Breda
Ryder, Dr Charles MAPM
Sadler, Rob MAPM
Samphire, Martin MAPM
Sanderson, Annmarie
Sarkar, Debashish
Savage, Michael MAPM
Scott, Andrew MAPM
Scott, Joanna MAPM

Scott, Lindsay MAPM
Scott, Noel
Semmons, Michael
Shannon, David HonFAPM
Shapley, Alex MAPM
Shaughnessy, Suzanne MAPM
Shaw, Lynn
Sheard, Kenneth MAPM
Shepherd, Miles HonFAPM
Sheikh, Naveed
Shreeve, Graham MAPM
Sidhu, Ranjit MAPM
Simister, Dr Steve RPP FAPM
Simon, Peter FAPM
Singha, Ashok Kumar MAPM
Smart, Alastair
Spencer, Peter MAPM
Somani, Sheilina FAPM
Stadnik, Raymond MAPM
Stollard, David MAPM
Sullivan, Markus MAPM
Summers, Eric MAPM
Syder, Steve RPP FAPM
Taggart, Adrian MAPM
Taylor, Andy FAPM
Taylor, Tom RPP HonFAPM
Taylorson, Lara RPP FAPM
Tillin, Adrian FAPM
Thomas, Bob MAPM
Thomas,Ian

Thomas, Jayne MAPM
Tomlinson, Mark MAPM
Tompkins, Karen
Turner, Dr Neil MAPM
Tsourapas, Thanos
Ugoji, Ngozi MAPM
Underhill, Elizabeth
Vivian, John FAPM
Vowler, Sue MAPM
Wake, Steve MAPM
Wallace, Michael MAPM
Waller, David
Wallington, Dr Edward
Walters, Chris MAPM
Warren, Tim
Wearne, Stephen HonFAPM
Wellings, Clive
Wells, Dominic MAPM
Wensley, Nick MAPM
Wernham, Brian RPP FAPM
Whitmore, David MAPM
Whyndham, Matthew MAPM
Williams, Graham MAPM
Williams, Dr Nigel L
Wilson, Liz
Wilson, Rachel
Wright, Derek MAPM
Wright, Moya MAPM
Wynn, Toni

APM Body of Knowledge 6th edition

Introduction

A body of knowledge is a complete set of concepts, terms and activities that make up a professional domain. The project management body of knowledge is created by practitioners, academics and authors from all areas of the economy. It has grown rapidly in scope over the last ten years, with new concepts increasing the breadth of the profession and new activities improving the practical application of those concepts.

Perhaps the most obvious increase in breadth is the development of programme management and portfolio management. Whilst it is convenient to pigeon-hole activity into one of the three dimensions of project, programme or portfolio, the reality is that these concepts are fluid and overlapping. Experienced practitioners should be able to draw upon techniques from all three dimensions in order to manage each unique package of work. Nonetheless, the term 'project management body of knowledge' no longer does justice to the broader reaches of the profession. It is partially because of this that the management of projects, programmes and portfolios is now commonly referred to as P3 Management.

Enforcing a standard terminology is difficult and sometimes counter-productive when the contributors to the body of knowledge are so varied. This document uses de-facto standard terms wherever possible and provides alternatives where necessary. Because this is the first document that endeavours to deal with project, programme and portfolio management as points on a continuum, some terminology has been adjusted to make that possible.

The increase in the conceptual breadth of the profession has inevitably been complemented by an increase in the depth of activity. The APM's first body of knowledge, published in 1992, was a collection of techniques that made up the profession. The vital role that these techniques play in all forms of modern commercial and non-commercial activity has led to an array of frameworks aimed at promoting and supporting successful application. The modern profession applies its component functions in the context of activities such as methodologies, competency frameworks, maturity models and qualifications. The overarching objective of this document is not to describe the entire body of knowledge in detail but to provide a guide and common structure for these activities.

It sets out to achieve this in three ways.

Firstly, by identifying topics using functional analysis. This approach focuses on the fundamental activities involved in project, programme and portfolio management rather than specific techniques or organisational structures. This creates a stable set of topics that will be less affected by the evolution of good practice.

Secondly, by adopting a hierarchical structure. Different levels of the structure will suit different types of activity. For example, whilst qualifications will be based on the lowest level of the structure, a maturity model will be based on higher level categories and a methodology will be a combination.

Thirdly, by adopting a matrix structure where the functions form one axis and the dimensions of project, programme and portfolio form the other. This allows a reader to consider all aspects of risk management on one dimension, or all aspects of programme management on the other.

This body of knowledge is the first one designed specifically to be used in electronic form. The style and structure lend themselves to being viewed according to the varying requirements of individuals and organisations.

This body of knowledge has been divided into four sections:

'Context' deals with the way that project, programme and portfolio management fits within the broader organisation.

'People' addresses the interpersonal skills and the nature of the profession.

'Delivery' is the section that covers the tools and techniques that are traditionally most associated with project, programme and portfolio management professionals.

'Interfaces' describes general management areas that are of particular importance to the project, programme or portfolio manager.

Project, programme and portfolio management

Project, programme and portfolio (P3) management is concerned with managing discrete packages of work to achieve objectives. The way the work is managed depends upon a wide variety of factors.

The scale, significance and complexity of the work are obvious factors: relocating a small office and organising the Olympics share many basic principles but offer very different managerial challenges.

Scale and complexity are not the only factors. Managing a major infrastructure development for delivery to a client will need a different approach to internally managing the merger of two banking organisations.

A good distinguishing factor is often to look at the nature of the objectives. Objectives may be expressed in terms of outputs (such as a new HQ building), outcomes (such as staff being relocated from multiple locations to the new HQ), benefits (such as reduced travel and facilities management costs) or strategic objectives (such as doubling the organisation's share price in three years).

Commonly, work of a lesser scale and complexity, leading to an output, is referred to as a project. Work that combines projects with change management to deliver benefits is considered to be a programme, while a collection of projects and programmes designed to achieve strategic objectives is called a portfolio.

However, some undertakings that only deliver outputs may be very large and complex, while some work that delivers benefits and encompasses the management of change may be relatively small and straightforward. Small organisations will have strategic portfolios that are nowhere near as complex and expensive as, say, a large government IT project.

Although projects, programmes and portfolios are often spoken of as being mutually exclusive approaches, they are actually just convenient combinations of managerial tools and techniques used to describe typical sets of circumstances.

The concept of projects, programmes and portfolios should be thought of as just points on a gradual scale of managing effort to deliver objectives.

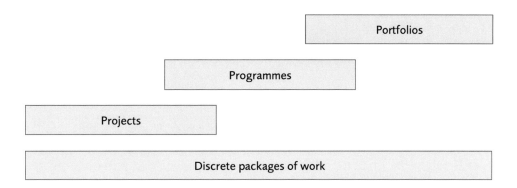

Figure 1: Scale of managing effort

Where appropriate, this body of knowledge looks at each topic from the perspective of the three domains: project, programme and portfolio. These are considered in the context of their 'typical' applications.

Someone who is new to these concepts will find it useful to be able to label undertakings as one or the other of the three levels. However, an experienced manager, working in a mature organisation, should be able to select different levels of tools and techniques from different topics to address the managerial needs of each package of work.

Mixing project-level scheduling with programme-level benefits management, for instance, may be entirely appropriate. Conceivably a single programme may constitute an entire portfolio.

This body of knowledge provides a flexible toolkit from which to select the most appropriate management approaches for any piece of work within the P3 domain.

Core texts

The books and websites cited here are relevant to most, if not all, of the sections in the *APM Body of Knowledge* and have been placed in the first section simply for convenience.

British Standards Institution, 2010.
BS 6079-1: 2010 A guide to project management. London: BSI.
[online] Available at: www.apm.org.uk/BoK6FurtherReading.

Burke, R., 2011.
Advanced project management. Ringwood: Burke Publishing.

Burke, R. and Barron, S., 2007.
Project management leadership. Ringwood: Burke Publishing.

Covey, S., 2004.
7 habits of highly effective people. London: Simon & Schuster.

International Organization for Standardization, (in press)
ISO 21500 guide to project management.

Linstead, S., Fulop, L. and Lilley, S., 2009.
Management and organisation, a critical text. Basingstoke: Palgrave Macmillan.

Morris, P., Pinto, J.K. and Soderlund, J. eds., 2011.
The Oxford handbook of project management. Oxford: Oxford University Press.

Office of Government Commerce, 2007.
Managing successful programmes. London: The Stationery Office.

Office of Government Commerce, 2008.
Portfolio, programme and project offices. Belfast: The Stationery Office.

Office of Government Commerce, 2009.
Directing successful projects with PRINCE2. London: The Stationery Office.

Office of Government Commerce, 2009.
Managing successful projects with PRINCE2. London: The Stationery Office.

Office of Government Commerce, 2010.
An executive guide to portfolio management. Norwich: The Stationery Office.

Office of Government Commerce, 2011.
Management of portfolios. London: The Stationery Office.

Project Management Institute, 2009.
A guide to the project management body of knowledge. 4th ed. Newtown Square, PA: Project Management Institute.

Remington, K. and Pollack, J., 2007.
Tools for complex projects. Aldershot: Gower.

Turner, J.R. ed., 2003.
People in project management. Aldershot: Gower.

Turner, R., 2008.
The Gower handbook of project management. 4th ed. Aldershot: Gower.

Turner, J.R., 2009.
The handbook of project based management, leading strategic change in organisations. 3rd ed. London: McGraw-Hill.

Turner, J.R. and Simister, S. eds., 2000.
Gower handbook of project management. 3rd ed. Aldershot: Gower.

Venning, C., 2007.
Managing portfolios of change with MSP for programmes and PRINCE2 for projects. London: The Stationery Office.

Weaver, R.G. and Farrell, J.D., 1997.
Managers as facilitators, a practical guide to getting work done in a changing workplace. San Francisco, CA: Berret-Koehler.

1 Context

The context of a project, programme or portfolio is made up of two areas: governance and setting.

Governance deals with the procedural and cultural aspects that need to be in place to improve the frequency and level of delivery success.

The topics covered here are the institutional factors that cannot be implemented overnight. An organisation that invests in this area over a period of years should consistently achieve higher levels of successful delivery.

Setting deals with the broad organisational factors that are outside the boundaries of the project, programme or portfolio but, nonetheless, have a significant impact upon the way the work is approached and carried out.

One important example of the setting is the sector in which the work is performed, e.g. IT, construction or defence. Another is the commercial nature of the work, e.g. for profit, not-for-profit, single or multi-organisational.

Whatever their sector or commercial setting, an organisation's projects, programmes and portfolios must be compatible with its overarching strategy and need to be compatible with the business-as-usual part of the organisation.

For internal delivery, a structured approach to change management ensures that beneficial changes are embedded within the organisation's operational approach. Where the work is performed on behalf of a client organisation, the contractor must also work within the client's environmental constraints.

The context of a portfolio (shown below) will always be the 'host organisation' e.g. a company, government department or charity. Some standalone programmes or projects will have the host organisation as their context, while some will be part of a portfolio. Equally, some projects will be part of a programme.

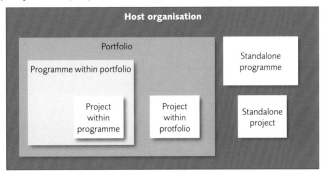

Figure 1.1: Context

1.1 Governance

Definition
Governance refers to the set of policies, regulations, functions, processes, procedures and responsibilities that define the establishment, management and control of projects, programmes and portfolios.

General
The governance of portfolios, programmes and projects is a necessary part of organisational governance. It gives an organisation the required internal controls while, externally, it reassures stakeholders that the money being spent is justified.

Good governance is increasingly demanded by shareholders, government and regulators. An organisation will often have to comply with external regulations and legislation (e.g. the UK Corporate Governance Code and Sarbanes-Oxley in the USA). The governance of projects, programmes and portfolios should support compliance in these areas.

The benefits of good P3 governance include the optimisation of investment, avoidance of common reasons for failure, and motivation of staff through better communication.

The application of good governance minimises risks arising from change and maximises the benefits. It also assures the continued development of the profession and disciplines of project, programme, and portfolio management.

Good governance can be demonstrated through:

- the adoption of a disciplined life cycle governance that includes approval gates at which viability is reviewed and approved;
- recording and communicating decisions made at approval gates;
- the acceptance of responsibility by the organisation's management board for P3 governance;
- establishing clearly defined roles, responsibilities and performance criteria for governance;
- developing coherent and supportive relationships between business strategy and P3;
- procedures that allow a management board to call for an independent scrutiny of projects, programmes and portfolios;
- fostering a culture of improvement and frank disclosure of P3 information;
- giving members of delegated bodies the capability and resources to make appropriate decisions;

- ensuring that business cases are supported by information that allows reliable decision-making;
- ensuring that stakeholders are engaged at a level that reflects their importance to the organisation and in a way that fosters trust;
- the deployment of suitably qualified and experienced people;
- ensuring that P3 management adds value.

In the case of a joint venture between two or more organisations, there should be:

- formally agreed governance arrangements covering unified decision-making and joint authority for managing contacts with owners, stakeholders and third parties;
- jointly agreed business cases that reflect the apportionment of risk and reward;
- arrangements for governance that take account of existing governance and the technical strengths and weaknesses of the co-owners;
- approval gates that give the owners the opportunity to re-evaluate their participation;
- agreed procedures for reporting, independent reviews and dispute resolution.

Virtually all topics within the body of knowledge contribute towards good governance. However, the key areas are:

- P3 management – the methodologies that deliver projects, programmes and portfolios;
- knowledge management – the organisation's ability to capture, develop and improve its capability to deliver;
- life cycle – the structure underpinning delivery;
- maturity – the development of increasing levels of capability;
- sponsorship – the link between P3, strategic management and business-as-usual;
- support – the support environment that provides P3 managers with consistency of practice.

As shown in figure 1.2, governance starts with the host organisation whose board must ensure that projects, programmes and portfolios are properly managed. The standards set by the board will be applied by a portfolio to its component programmes and projects. A programme will be responsible for applying the standards to its component projects.

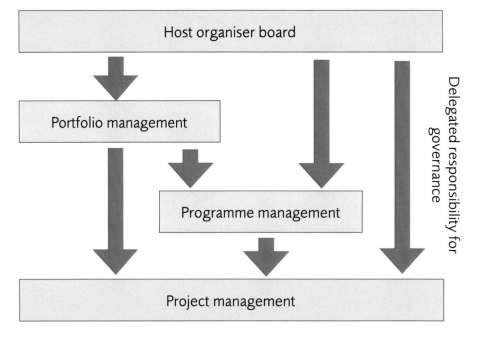

Figure 1.2: Governance structure

Project

In a less mature organisation, where such centrally driven governance is not in place, the project team will have to take responsibility for governance themselves.

The project sponsor is responsible for ensuring that adequate governance mechanisms are in place. Periodically checking that governance mechanisms are being applied is referred to as project assurance. This should be performed by someone external to the project management team and who reports to the project sponsor.

Programme

Where a programme is part of a portfolio, it will adhere to the governance standards set by the portfolio. If the programme has been created as a stand-alone entity, then it may need to create its own governance mechanisms.

Sometimes programmes are formed partly from existing projects that may not be managed in a consistent manner. The programme management team then has the added challenge of changing project governance part way through existing projects. The risk of allowing projects to continue unchanged has to be balanced against the benefits of adopting a consistent approach across the programme.

A programme assurance function will report to the programme sponsor to ensure that governance standards are being applied. This will also include conducting project assurance on the component projects.

Portfolio

Some organisations will simply have one portfolio comprising all the programmes and projects they undertake. The governance of the portfolio will then drive the governance of all projects and programmes.

Larger organisations may have several portfolios divided by geography, operating division, or subsidiary. There may be compelling reasons for having different governance frameworks in these different portfolios. This may arise from varying cultural or regulatory environments, but the core values should be consistent across the organisation and compatible with organisational governance.

Portfolio assurance will be conducted by a corporate quality function reporting to the body that provides portfolio sponsorship.

Further Reading

APM Governance of Project Management Specific Interest Group, 2007.
Co-directing change: a guide to the governance of multi-owned projects. Princes Risborough: Association for Project Management.

APM Governance of Project Management Specific Interest Group, 2009.
Sponsoring change: a guide to the governance aspects of project sponsorship. Princes Risborough: Association for Project Management.

APM Governance of Project Management Specific Interest Group, 2011.
Directing change: a guide to governance of project management. 2nd ed. Princes Risborough: Association for Project Management.

Reiss, G. et al., 2006.
The Gower handbook of programme management. London: Gower.

1.1.1 Project management

Definition

Project management is the application of processes, methods, knowledge, skills and experience to achieve the project objectives.

General

A project is a unique, transient endeavour, undertaken to achieve planned objectives, which could be defined in terms of outputs, outcomes or benefits. A project is usually deemed to be a success if it achieves the objectives according to their acceptance criteria, within an agreed timescale and budget.

The core components of project management are:

- defining the reason why a project is necessary;
- capturing project requirements, specifying quality of the deliverables, estimating resources and timescales;
- preparing a business case to justify the investment;
- securing corporate agreement and funding;
- developing and implementing a management plan for the project;
- leading and motivating the project delivery team;
- managing the risks, issues and changes on the project;
- monitoring progress against plan;
- managing the project budget;
- maintaining communications with stakeholders and the project organisation;
- provider management;
- closing the project in a controlled fashion when appropriate.

Responsibility for these components lies with a project sponsor and a project manager. The project sponsor is accountable for achievement of the business case and providing senior-level commitment to the project.

The project manager is responsible for day-to-day management of the project and must be competent in managing the six aspects of a project, i.e. scope, schedule, finance, risk, quality and resources. Well-developed interpersonal skills such as leadership, communication and conflict management are also vitally important.

Investment in effective project management will have a number of benefits to both the host organisation and the people involved in delivering the project. It will:

- provide a greater likelihood of achieving the desired result;
- ensure efficient and best value use of resources;
- satisfy the differing needs of the project's stakeholders.

A project management methodology can be used to support the governance structure for management of a project. Such methodologies typically include:

- process models based around a project life cycle;
- an organisation structure with defined roles;
- templates for documentation;
- guidelines for adapting the methodology to different situations.

The benefits of using a standard methodology across an organisation include:

- use of consistent terminology;
- a common understanding of the responsibilities associated with roles;
- consistent documentation across projects;
- a structure for development of new project managers;
- greater mobility of staff between projects.

Many organisations either tailor open methodologies (such as PRINCE2™) or develop their own bespoke approaches.

A methodology can be applied in conjunction with a development method such as waterfall or agile. The former is a sequential, staged development process, whereas the latter provides an iterative and incremental development process. The traditional waterfall approach concentrates on gathering full requirements at the outset, and then calculating the time and resource required to deliver them. Agile focuses on which requirements can be delivered in a certain time with the resources available.

Further reading

Project Management Association of Japan, 2005.
A guidebook for project and program management for enterprise innovation "P2M".
[online] Available at: www.apm.org.uk/BoK6FurtherReading.

1.1.2 Programme management

Definition

Programme management is the coordinated management of projects and change management activities to achieve beneficial change.

General

A programme usually starts with a vision of a changed organisation and the benefits that will accrue from the change. Delivering the changed organisation will involve coordinating a number of projects and ensuring that their outputs are used to deliver benefits. This will require change management of business-as-usual activities.

Typically, the desired benefits are initially identified within a business case that justifies the necessary investment. A detailed specification of the end state of the programme is called a blueprint. However, the scale of programmes and the impact of a dynamic business environment mean that intermittent or regular redefinition may be required.

The core programme management processes are:

- project coordination: identifying, initiating, accelerating, decelerating, redefining and terminating projects within the programme. Managing interdependencies between projects, and between projects and business-as-usual activities;
- transformation: taking project outputs and managing change within business-as-usual so that outputs deliver outcomes;
- benefits management: defining, quantifying, measuring and monitoring benefits;
- stakeholder management and communications: ensuring that relationships are developed and maintained, thus enabling productive, two-way communication with all key stakeholders.

Responsibility for these components lies with three key roles: a programme sponsor, a programme manager and business change managers.

The sponsor is accountable for achievement of the business case and providing senior-level commitment to the programme.

The programme manager is responsible for day-to-day management of the programme including the coordination of projects and change management activities.

Business change managers are responsible for successful transition and benefits realisation.

A programme management methodology can be used to provide the complete governance structure for management of a programme. Such methodologies typically provide:

- process models based around a programme life cycle;

- an organisation structure with defined roles and responsibilities;
- templates for documentation;
- guidelines for adapting the methodology to different situations.

The benefits of using a methodology for programmes are the same as for projects. Ideally, the projects within the programme will all use a common (but flexible) methodology that is consistent with the programme's methodology.

Many organisations either tailor open methodologies, such as Managing Successful Programmes (MSP™), or develop their own bespoke approaches.

Corporate programmes tend to be complex, lengthy and initially ambiguous as to the eventual outcomes. Instability within an organisation's environment (e.g. market changes) can often affect the outcomes envisaged for the end of a programme.

In order to balance the cumulative impact of changes, a programme should be divided into tranches. The programme can then be reviewed at the end of each tranche. Ideally, each tranche should deliver a self-sustainable amount of beneficial change in its own right.

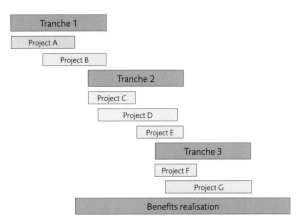

Figure 1.3: Programme tranches

Further reading

Reiss, G. et al., 2006.
The Gower handbook of programme management. London: Gower.

Bartlett, J., 2010.
Managing programmes of business change. 5th ed. Hook: Project Manager Today.

Williams, D. and Parr, T., 2006.
Enterprise programme management: delivering value. revised ed. Basingstoke: Palgrave Macmillan.

Thiry, M., 2010.
Programme management. Aldershot: Gower.

1.1.3 Portfolio management

Definition

Portfolio management is the selection, prioritisation and control of an organisation's projects and programmes in line with its strategic objectives and capacity to deliver. The goal is to balance change initiatives and business-as-usual while optimising return on investment.

General

Portfolios can be managed at an organisational or functional level and address three questions:

■ Are these the projects and programmes needed to deliver the strategic objectives, subject to risk, resource constraints and affordability?
■ Is the organisation delivering them effectively and efficiently?
■ Are the full potential benefits from the organisation's investment being realised?

The portfolio life cycle encompasses techniques such as:

■ strategic planning;
■ change management;
■ project and programme management.

The portfolio life cycle encompasses such techniques such as:

■ segmenting the portfolio into categories and tailoring the investment criteria accordingly;
■ portfolio prioritisation based on assessments of risk and return;
■ assessments of progress via stage gates;
■ periodic portfolio-level reviews and regular portfolio reporting;
■ consistent portfolio-wide approaches to benefits management.

The portfolio management process must constantly review the balance of investment and benefit, creating and closing projects and programmes as necessary. This will include prematurely closing projects or programmes where they are no longer viable.
    The benefits of applying a portfolio approach include:

■ maintaining a balanced and strategically aligned portfolio in the context of changing conditions;

- improved delivery of projects and programmes through a portfolio-wide view of risk, dependencies, and scheduling to reflect the capacity of different parts of the organisation to absorb change;
- reduced costs by removing overlapping, poorly performing and non-strategically aligned projects and programmes;
- more efficient and effective use of limited resources, by matching demand and supply, and optimising allocation of available resources;
- increased realisation of forecast benefits and the identification and realisation of unplanned benefits to create additional value.

Achieving these benefits is dependent on repeatable processes supported by:

- a clearly articulated strategy;
- senior management commitment to, and active championing of, the portfolio management processes to ensure that stakeholders collaborate in pursuit of shared goals;
- a clear governance structure that is understood by stakeholders;
- a portfolio management office function to provide impartial and credible analysis and decision-making support to the portfolio management team, along with support to projects and programmes.

Good governance of an organisation's portfolio provides an opportunity to improve the management of projects and programmes consistently. A well-managed portfolio provides the structure and commitment needed to improve an organisation or function's maturity.

Further reading

Benko, C. and McFarlane, W., 2003.
Connecting the dots: aligning projects with objectives in unpredictable times.
Boston, MA: Harvard Business School Press.

Office of Government Commerce, 2010.
An executive guide to portfolio management. Norwich: The Stationery Office.

Office of Government Commerce, 2011.
Management of portfolios. London: The Stationery Office.

Sanwal, A., 2007.
Optimising corporate portfolio management. Hoboken, NJ: Wiley.

1.1.4 Infrastructure

Definition

Infrastructure provides support for projects, programmes and portfolios, and is the focal point for the development and maintenance of P3 management within an organisation.

General

The governance of P3 management requires a permanent organisational infrastructure that supports the temporary organisational structures of projects, programmes and portfolios.

Many different names are given to the structures that 'own' P3 management within an organisation. The terms EPMO (Enterprise Project Management Office), PSO (Project, Programme or Portfolio Support Office), Project Services or Centre of Excellence are all in common use.

The name often reflects the scope of responsibilities. For example, a Project Support Office will provide predominantly administrative support to a project, while a Centre of Excellence will often be responsible for improving P3 management maturity.

Routine administration is required on all projects, programmes and portfolios. On small projects this may be performed by the project manager, but on medium to large projects and all programmes and portfolios, a P3 manager needs support in handling day-to-day administration.

Some projects and most programmes and portfolios also require specialist skills in areas such as risk, quality or finance.

An administrative support function can operate at different levels depending upon how it is constituted. It may provide:

- administrative help in areas such as planning, risk management, change control etc.;
- the secretariat for meetings and logistical services for members of the management team;
- technical support including collecting, analysing and presenting progress information, managing interdependencies and handling communications with stakeholders;
- assurance of governance structures and standard project management practices through audits, health checks and phase end reviews.

A sophisticated infrastructure may also cover:

- provision of subject matter expertise to ensure that there is access to all necessary tools and techniques;
- training, coaching and mentoring for the project, programme or portfolio management team;
- maintaining the infrastructure, momentum and drive to support communities of practice;
- improving, embedding and measuring capabilities to achieve higher levels of maturity;
- owning and deploying standard tools and techniques.

The P3 management infrastructure may range from a single person to a large team containing many different roles and specialists including, among others:

- planners and schedulers;
- cost engineers;
- subject matter experts;
- assurance staff;
- configuration managers.

The overall infrastructure may be divided into multiple offices, some temporary and some permanent. For example, a support office might provide administrative support to a specific project or programme. This is then disbanded once the work is complete. In contrast, a community of practice, or centre of excellence, has a permanent support role independent of the creation and completion of any individual piece of work.

The shape of the infrastructure will reflect its environment, but its component groups must always have a clearly defined purpose and scope. The roles and levels of authority of these groups must be communicated to the delivery team(s) and reinforced periodically.

Project

In the project dimension, the main focus is on administrative and technical support. Where a project is part of a programme or portfolio, the project support function will be provided by the programme or portfolio office.

On smaller, stand-alone projects that cannot justify the overhead of a support function, the support work will fall on the project manager's shoulders. This can lead to a reaction against 'bureaucracy' when the project manager is asked to spend a lot of time producing standard documentation. Some organisations will have central

functions for planning, cost management, procurement etc., that may be able to provide assistance in these circumstances.

With the support of the sponsor, the project manager of a small, stand-alone project should seek as much help with day-to-day administration as possible. Taking shortcuts in the administration of even the smallest project is often a cause of failure.

Beyond day-to-day management of the project, the project manager should be provided with other types of support. This may include continuing professional development (CPD) through communities of practice, career advice or managing the transition between one project and the next. It is this broad support for the profession and discipline of project management that is provided by the governance infrastructure.

Programme

Programmes are large enough to carry the overhead of a support function and may also have access to a central support function.

Programme support functions must have the expertise to cover the additional services required by programmes. These typically include supporting change management, benefits realisation and project interfaces.

The programme management team decide how to constitute the support organisation across the programme, e.g. whether one support function will serve the programme and all its component projects, or whether some, or all, projects will have separate project support functions.

Portfolio

Some organisations will have multiple departmental or regional portfolios, while others might have a single, organisation-wide portfolio. In the latter case, the portfolio and the governance infrastructure are effectively the same thing. This is often referred to as an EPMO and is a permanent organisational structure.

Further reading

Refer to core texts on pages 4–5.

1.1.5 Knowledge management

Definition

Knowledge management is the systematic management of information and learning. It turns personal information and experience into collective knowledge that can be widely shared throughout an organisation and a profession.

General

Organisations need to capture knowledge and experience, optimise their usefulness and make them available to improve decision-making. This way they can avoid repeating mistakes of the past. Knowledge management underpins organisational learning and maturity.

Knowledge is all-encompassing. It can come from both external and internal sources, ranging from published standards and methods to books and conferences. However, a primary source of knowledge comes from experience developed within an organisation.

An organisation will often document its own experience as 'lessons learned'. These are captured both formally and informally but, all too often, are not distilled into a format that can be easily used by others.

The key steps involved in ensuring that knowledge is captured and shared include:

- establishing ownership of knowledge management and the systems that support it;
- implementing mechanisms for finding external knowledge and making it relevant internally;
- identification and extraction of key lessons from projects, programmes and portfolios, including contextual information;
- structuring and storing knowledge so that it can be accessed easily;
- maintenance of the knowledge repository to ensure it is up to date;
- embedding processes that ensure knowledge is used effectively.

Knowledge management may be a corporate function, with P3 management being simply one aspect of a broader organisational learning strategy. However, if P3 knowledge management is owned separately, then it may reside in a P3 support function or in communities of practice.

Wherever P3 knowledge management is located, it must be made easily available. This entails the creation and maintenance of a knowledge 'database' that can be interrogated for each project, programme or portfolio.

There are two key challenges: knowledge is difficult to assemble and it is difficult to encourage its use.

Many managers see it as a time-consuming distraction from their core role. This means that P3 management must include procedures for capturing knowledge at the inception of each new piece of work and as it is being undertaken.

Learning from experience must become second nature to all those involved and assurance processes should check that this is the case.

Knowledge capture should occur:

- during governance meetings (e.g. board and delivery team meetings);
- during reviews (e.g. gateway, closure and benefits reviews);
- during third party meetings;
- during an assurance audit;
- at any time that an important lesson is learned.

Knowledge should be used:

- at inception (e.g. to help develop a robust business case);
- during mobilisation to help define the governance approach;
- during reviews to identify solutions to problems;
- at all times to improve personal and team performance.

Good knowledge management can reduce risks and increase efficiency through the re-use of proven approaches and avoidance of known pitfalls. It can also produce a virtuous circle as individuals and teams see their contributions recognised and re-used, thus encouraging further participation in the process.

Project

In a mature organisation, project teams will have access to a knowledge base of lessons learned and an accepted process for incorporating them into a new project.

Where a project stands alone, the project manager needs to take the initiative. This could involve simply speaking to other project managers to glean experience, or researching similar projects.

Simple actions, such as keeping a project diary with particular emphasis on lessons learned, can improve the efficiency and effectiveness of project management.

Programme

A programme, by definition, contains multiple projects. This creates the opportunity to capture lessons from earlier projects and apply them to the management of later projects.

The programme team should factor into their plans the overhead of managing knowledge and encourage the project teams to contribute.

Portfolio

Consistency of knowledge management across the portfolio is a significant contributor to developing organisational maturity.

A portfolio often includes all the projects and programmes within the host organisation. Implementing an effective knowledge management system at the portfolio level effectively improves the P3 maturity of the whole organisation.

Portfolio management teams should secure the funding for knowledge management within the portfolio where such a system does not already exist.

Further reading

"British Standards Institution, 2001.
PAS 2001:2001 knowledge management: a guide to good practice. London: BSI.
[online] Available at: www.apm.org.uk/BoK6FurtherReading

British Standards Institution, 2003.
PD 7501:2003 managing culture and knowledge: a guide to good practice. London:
BSI.
[online] Available at: www.apm.org.uk/BoK6FurtherReading

British Standards Institution, 2003.
PD 7502:2003 guide to measurements in knowledge management. London: BSI.
[online] Available at: www.apm.org.uk/BoK6FurtherReading

British Standards Institution, 2005.
*PD 7506:2005 linking knowledge management with other organizational functions
and disciplines. A guide to good practice*. London: BSI
 [online] Available at: www.apm.org.uk/BoK6FurtherReading

European Committee for Standardization, 2004.
*CWA 14924-4:2004 European guide to good practice in knowledge management,
guidelines for measuring KM*. CEN.

European Committee for Standardization, 2004.
*CWA 14924-5:2004 European guide to good practice in knowledge management,
KM terminology*. CEN.

Office of Government Commerce, 2008.
Portfolio, programme and project offices. Belfast: The Stationery Office.

1.1.6 Life cycle

Definition

A life cycle defines the inter-related phases of a project, programme or portfolio and provides a structure for governing the progression of the work.

General

All projects, programmes and portfolios are designed to deliver objectives. These objectives may be expressed as outputs, outcomes or benefits. A P3 life cycle illustrates the distinct phases that take an initial idea, develop it into detailed objectives and then deliver those objectives.

All life cycles follow a similar high-level generic sequence but this can be expressed in quite different ways. Life cycles will differ across industries and business sectors.

The most common type is the linear life cycle, sometimes known as the linear sequential model or waterfall method. In addition to the linear model, other life cycle formats include:

- parallel – this is similar to the linear, but phases are carried out in parallel to increase the pace of delivery;
- spiral – this is often employed where many options, requirements and constraints are unknown at the start (e.g. in prototyping or research projects);
- 'v' – this is applied in software development where requirements are defined and the development tools are well known.

The phased structure facilitates the creation of governance and feedback mechanisms:

- stages – development work can be further subdivided into a series of management stages (usually referred to as 'tranches' in programmes) with work being authorised one stage at a time;
- gate reviews – these are conducted at the end of a phase, stage or tranche. Senior management will consider performance to date and plans for the next phase, stage or tranche before deciding whether it is viable;
- post-reviews – learning from experience is a key factor in maturity. Post-project and programme reviews document lessons learned for use in the future;
- benefit reviews – these measure the achievement of benefits against the business case.

All phases of the life cycle are important. No phase should be omitted but they may be adjusted to accommodate the development methodology and context of the work.

Project

The scope of a project life cycle can take various forms to suit the context. Some projects will be part of a programme and will only be concerned with delivering outputs (the traditional project life cycle). Some projects will be expected to incorporate the management of change and realisation of benefits (the extended project life cycle). Some applications (e.g. whole life costing) may consider the full product life cycle.

Where a contractor is working for a client, the contractor's 'project' may simply be the development, handover and closure phases of the client's project that will include benefits realisation.

A typical, linear project life cycle is shown in figure 1.4 below:

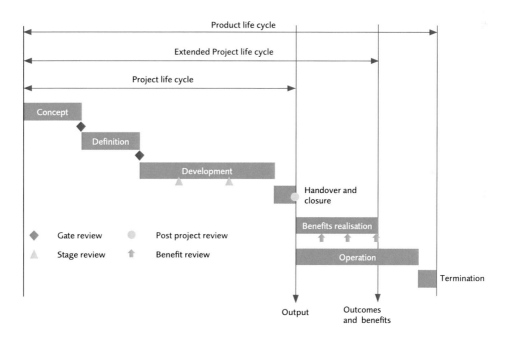

Figure 1.4: Linear project life cycle

■ Concept – this phase develops an initial idea and creates an outline business case and schedule. A sponsor is appointed and, if possible, a project manager. Sufficient analysis must be performed to enable senior managers, led by the project sponsor, to make two decisions:
  ■ Is the project likely to be viable?
  ■ Is it definitely worth investing in the definition phase?

- Definition – the preferred solution is identified and ways of achieving it are refined. The project management plan (PMP) is developed. This, together with the business case, has to be approved by the sponsor before progressing to the next phase.
- Development – the project management plan is put into action and this phase may be broken down into further stages at the end of which the continuing viability of the project can be reviewed.
- Handover and closure – the project outputs are handed over and accepted by the sponsor on behalf of the users.
- Benefits realisation – where appropriate, a project may include a benefits realisation phase.

The full product life cycle also includes:

- operation – continuing support and maintenance;
- termination – closure at the end of the product's useful life.

Programme

A typical programme life cycle is shown in figure 1.5.

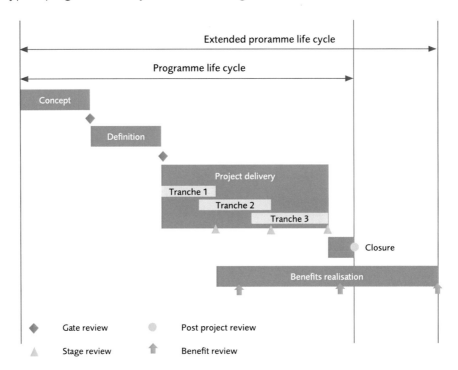

Figure 1.5: Linear programme life cycle

- Concept – this establishes the vision and outline business case for the programme. A programme board is created to oversee the phase and provide a mechanism for approvals. The expected benefits are outlined and initial programme-level documentation is prepared. Sufficient analysis must be performed to enable the programme board, led by the programme sponsor, to make two decisions:
  - Is the programme likely to be viable?
  - Is it definitely worth investing in the definition phase
- Definition – the vision is developed into a detailed specification of the end state of the programme, sometimes referred to as a blueprint. Outline plans and business case are further developed so that the sponsor can make an informed decision to proceed with the programme.
- Project delivery – this phase is usually broken into groups of projects called tranches that deliver beneficial change in their own right. A review at the end of each tranche assesses the continuing viability of the programme.
- Benefits realisation – as new outputs are delivered by projects, transformation work has to be done to ensure new ways of working become embedded in business-as-usual. Benefits will be measured and compared to the baseline in the business case.
- Closure – closure of the last projects, closure of budgets and disbanding the programme management team.

The realisation of benefits will usually continue after the closure of the programme. Some members of the programme team (typically the programme sponsor and business change managers) will continue in their roles to ensure that benefits are realised as required by the business case.

Portfolio

Unlike projects and programmes, portfolios are less likely to have a defined start and finish. Portfolio management is a more continual cycle coordinating projects and programmes. It may, however, be constrained by a strategic planning cycle that reviews strategy over a defined period. If an organisation has, for example, a three-year strategic planning cycle, then the portfolio cycle will have a start and finish within that period.

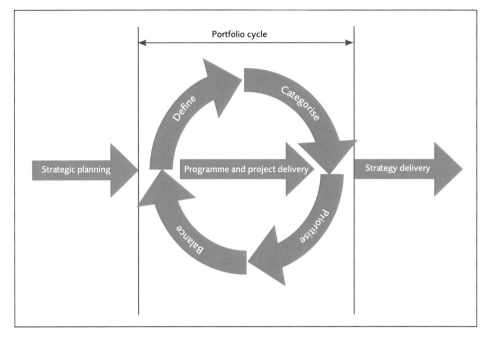

Figure 1.6: Portfolio life cycle

The objectives of a portfolio are created by strategic planning. The aim of the portfolio is to deliver the objectives and realise the corporate strategy through the coordination of projects and programmes.

The phases of the portfolio life cycle are less likely to be linear. At any point in time the emphasis will be on one phase or another, but aspects of all may be undertaken.

- Define – the projects, programmes and change to business-as-usual required to meet strategic objectives are identified and evaluated in a selection process that maximises the effectiveness of the portfolio.
- Categorise – the projects and programmes may be organised into 'sub-portfolios' or groups that share certain characteristics, such as alignment with particular strategic objectives.
- Prioritise – priorities can be set by strategic objective, return on investment or any other chosen metric. On the assumption that no organisation has sufficient resource to do everything it wants, the prioritisation process forms the basis of the next phase.
- Balance – the portfolio must be balanced in terms of risk, resource usage, cash flow and impact across the business.

Portfolio management may incorporate the overall governance of projects and programmes within an organisation. The portfolio management team may be responsible not only for coordinating the projects and programmes, but also for improving the maturity of project and programme management.

Further Reading

Frigenti, E. and Comninos, D., 2002.
The practice of project management: a guide to the business-focused approach. London: Kogan Page.

Gardiner, P.D., 2005.
Project management, a strategic planning approach. Basingstoke: Palgrave Macmillan.

Reiss, G. et al., 2006.
The Gower handbook of programme management. London: Gower.

1.1.7 Success factors and maturity

Definition

Success factors are management practices that, when implemented, will increase the likelihood of success of a project, programme or portfolio. The degree to which these practices are established and embedded within an organisation indicates its level of maturity.

General

There are many recognised factors that are known to contribute to success. Their presence in a project, programme or portfolio does not in itself guarantee success, but their absence will contribute to its failure. Some high-level success factors include:

- defining clear goals and objectives;
- maintaining a focus on business value;
- implementing a proper governance structure;
- ensuring senior management commitment;
- providing timely and clear communication.

These success factors can be collected together to form a framework that not only describes an organisational environment in which success is the norm, but also provides a mechanism to help organisations improve.

A maturity model identifies the stages in an organisation's development from its initial chaotic attempts to manage projects, programmes and portfolios, to a point where most initiatives succeed and the organisation has the ability to improve continuously.

Most models are based on the Capability Maturity Model (CMM) originally developed at Carnegie Mellon University. This identifies five levels of progression:

Level 1 - Initial: the delivery process is ad hoc and occasionally chaotic. Few processes are defined and success depends upon individual effort and heroics.

Level 2 - Repeatable: basic processes are established and the necessary discipline is in place to repeat earlier successes.

Level 3 - Defined: processes are documented and standardised. All projects, programmes or portfolios use an approved, tailored version of the documented processes.

Level 4 - Managed: metrics are gathered on process performance and used to control future performance.

Level 5 - Optimising: continuous process improvement is enabled by quantitative feedback from the process and from piloting innovative ideas and technologies. In the P3 management environment, an organisation's maturity can be defined separately for projects, programmes and portfolios, i.e. an organisation may be at level 3 for the management of projects but only at level 2 for the management of programmes.

Maturity may be further divided into key process areas such as:

- scope;
- schedule;
- finance;
- risk;
- quality;
- resource.

This enables an organisation to assess and develop maturity in particular areas such as project risk management or programme resource management.

Each area has a number of attributes that are indicative of the level of maturity. For example, a well-known success factor is that risks should be identified, assessed and acted upon. The relevant attributes that indicate an organisation's level of maturity may then be:

- Level 1: risks arbitrarily classified and rarely, if ever, quantified;
- Level 2: some projects recognise different categories of risk;
- Level 3: risks identified, assessed and controlled in accordance with recognised procedures, across all projects;
- Level 4: projects able to demonstrate resource and budgetary implications of risks throughout the project life cycle;
- Level 5: risk assessment underpins all decision-making.

If an organisation wishes to deliver projects, programmes and portfolios effectively and efficiently, it should aspire to level 3 and upwards. This requires serious commitment from senior management to establish the maturity of the organisation, benchmark against a standard model (such as P3M3) and implement planned improvements.

Project

Projects are the basic building blocks of both programmes and portfolios and many organisations start to develop their maturity by addressing success factors in the project environment. It is highly unlikely that an organisation could start to develop a mature approach to delivering programmes and portfolios without first establishing a consistent way of managing projects.

Programme

Ideally, programmes are initiated in an organisational environment where project management is already well established and consistent. However, it is not uncommon for an organisation to be managing projects in an inconsistent manner and then collect these together in a programme.

In this instance the programme management team has an opportunity to develop programme-wide governance mechanisms for the component projects. In this way, programmes can not only deliver defined organisational change and benefits, but also act as a catalyst for improving the maturity of project management which in itself leads towards programme management maturity.

Portfolio

Achieving maturity in portfolio management first requires the development of maturity in project and programme management.

The scale of portfolios means that they have an important role to play in embedding mature practices in the project and programme domains. The portfolio management team can provide the continuing drive to improve project and programme delivery that leads to the 'managed' and 'optimising' levels of maturity. Similarly, over several cycles of strategic planning, the executive board of the organisation are the ones who must drive maturity in portfolio management.

Further reading

Refer to core texts on pages 4–5.

1.1.8 Sponsorship

Definition
Sponsorship of a project, programme or portfolio is an important senior management role. The sponsor is accountable for ensuring that the work is governed effectively and delivers the objectives that meet identified needs.

General
Sponsorship is normally carried out by an individual who may also be known as an executive, senior responsible owner (SRO) or client.

A sponsor may be supported by other senior managers. They will be referred to as a P3 board or steering group. Even if there is a board, the sponsor is still accountable and needs to continue to play an active sponsorship role.

The sponsor owns the business case. There must be a close relationship between the sponsor and the P3 manager to ensure that the business case remains viable. Will it deliver the defined outputs and benefits? If the value of predicted benefits no longer exceeds the cost or risk of achieving them, a sponsor must work with the P3 manager to redefine or prematurely close the project, programme or portfolio.

The P3 manager is accountable to the sponsor. They need a continuous dialogue to ensure a common understanding of the:

- work to be done;
- benefits sought;
- cost and risk of delivering the benefits.

It is vital that the sponsor and manager should have a good working relationship and operate as a team. The sponsor will support the P3 manager, for example, in dealing with issues and communicating with more senior stakeholders.

A communication management plan will clearly state communication responsibilities and a robust control system will identify issues that need to be escalated from the manager to the sponsor.

A sponsor needs to be:

- a business leader and decision-maker with the credibility to work across corporate and functional boundaries;
- an enthusiastic advocate of the work and the change it brings about;
- prepared to commit time and support to the role;
- sufficiently experienced in P3 to judge if the work is being managed effectively and to challenge P3 managers where appropriate.

APM Body of Knowledge 6th edition

Project

The role of the project sponsor starts before the appointment of the project manager. It continues beyond project closure and the departure of the project manager.

As owner of the business case, the project sponsor is responsible for overseeing the delivery of the benefits. So the sponsorship role covers the whole project life cycle.

The project sponsorship role will often be taken by the programme manager where the project is part of a programme.

The sponsor and the project manager may be from different organisations. In a contractual situation the sponsor will typically be from a client organisation and the project manager from a contracting organisation.

The latter adds a layer of complexity because the client's sponsor and the contractor's manager will have separate commercial objectives. In this situation it is advisable to have a senior contractor representative on a project board working with the sponsor.

Programme

The scale of programmes will often require a sponsor to be supported by a group of senior managers who perform some sponsorship duties. However, ultimate accountability will lie with the programme sponsor.

Programmes include the management of change in business-as-usual activities. The programme sponsor must have the authority and credibility to carry through change that will often be difficult. There is inevitably opposition to change and the sponsor will need excellent communication and influencing skills to ensure realisation of the benefits in the business case.

The programme manager should also be a competent project sponsor and will often perform that role for some, or all, of the programme's component projects.

Portfolio

Sponsorship of a portfolio of projects and programmes will be undertaken by a senior executive with the necessary status, credibility and authority. This may well be a main board member, or even the CEO of the organisation. The scale of a portfolio will require an extensive governance organisation. This may involve, for example, committees with the responsibility for investment decisions or management of change.

The sponsor must ensure that the portfolio remains aligned with the strategic direction of the organisation, and secure the necessary funding and resources.

To do this the portfolio sponsor needs to provide high-profile leadership and be able to communicate effectively at a strategic level.

1 Context

Further reading

APM Governance of Project Management Specific Interest Group, 2007. *Co-directing change: a guide to the governance of multi-owned projects*. Princes Risborough: Association for Project Management.

APM Governance of Project Management Specific Interest Group, 2009. *Sponsoring change: a guide to the governance aspects of project sponsorship*. Princes Risborough: Association for Project Management.

APM Governance of Project Management Specific Interest Group, 2011. *Directing change: a guide to governance of project management*. 2nd ed. Princes Risborough: Association for Project Management.

Office of Government Commerce, 2009. *Directing successful projects with PRINCE2*. London: The Stationery Office.

1.2 **Setting**

Definition
The relationship of the project, programme or portfolio with its host organisation.

General
Projects, programmes and portfolios do not exist in isolation. P3 management is influenced by its environment and works closely with other broad management disciplines.

Every project, programme or portfolio has a host organisation. That organisation will apply strategic management to set out its goals and reason for existence. It will then deliver its core products and services through operations management. Strategic planning will take into account the organisation's environment which, in conjunction with chosen methods for delivering the strategy, will govern the P3 environment.

This section explains the key characteristics of strategic management and operations management and how they relate to P3 management. It also explains the many environmental factors that will influence the way that a project, programme or portfolio is constituted and managed.

Further reading
Refer to core texts on pages 4–5.

1.2.1 Environment

Definition
The circumstances and conditions within which the project, programme or portfolio must operate.

General
The way a project, programme or portfolio is constituted and managed will depend upon many different environmental factors. These must be understood by the P3 sponsor and manager at the outset so that the work is managed in an appropriate manner.

Projects are often delivered by a contracting organisation for a client, while others are managed in-house. In the former situation the contracting organisation is given a specification for an output and its involvement ends with the handover of the completed deliverables.

The contractor's project may well be a sub-set of the client's project or programme. In this case the way the work is managed is greatly influenced by the contractual terms agreed at the start of the work.

Major projects or programmes may be beyond the scope of any one organisation. This often requires the creation of joint ventures where the two or more partner organisations seek to achieve common objectives. This can make funding, apportionment of benefits and stakeholder management much more complex.

Projects, programmes and portfolios exist in the public and private sectors and may be for commercial or not-for-profit organisations. This aspect of the environment has a great influence on how risk, innovation and value are perceived.

These are only some of the multitude of factors that make up the P3 environment. Others may include those relating to:

- the commercial sector, i.e. construction, IT, engineering, pharmaceuticals, etc.;
- international work, perhaps with multiple geographical locations and operational languages;
- regulated environments where outputs, outcomes, benefits and the way work is performed must conform to specific standards;
- the public sector and its need for accountability and transparency.

All these factors occur in infinite combinations and each will have a unique effect on the way a project, programme or portfolio is set up and managed.

The P3 sponsor or manager needs to perform an assessment of the environment as early as possible in the life cycle. Of the typical 'checklists' that exist to help such an assessment, the most common is PESTLE, which stands for political, economic, sociological, technical, legal and ecological factors.

The assessment should not only consider the effect that the environment has on the project, programme or portfolio. It should also consider the impact of the work on its environment.

As the work progresses, the interactions between the work and its environment will develop and change. The P3 sponsor and manager must monitor this relationship and identify any threats and opportunities that arise.

Further reading

Refer to core texts on pages 4–5.

1.2.2 Operations management

Definition

Operations management relates to the management of those activities that create the core services or products provided by an organisation.

General

Operations management was originally developed in product-based industries, but the principles have been adapted to service-based organisations. In the context of P3 management, operations management is viewed as the activity that is affected by, but does not form part of, a project, programme or portfolio.

In simple terms, operations management manages routine activity, while P3 management implements change. For this reason, the activities covered by operations management are often collectively termed, from the P3 perspective, as 'business-as-usual'.

Operations management is concerned with the conversion of inputs into outputs under management control. It will have many different components depending on the nature of the organisation. Figure 1.7 shows some examples of the range of possible components.

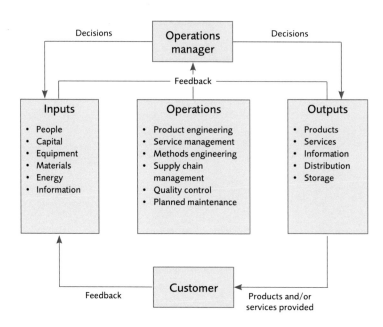

Figure 1.7: Operations management

As with P3 management, business-as-usual activities will be supported by disciplines such as HR management, marketing, legal and financial.

One of the first steps in organisational P3 management maturity is the ability to differentiate what should be managed as business-as-usual and what should be managed as a project or programme. This is not always an obvious distinction.

Some packages of work (for example, in planned maintenance) may meet the definition of a project, but be more easily managed as a component of operations management.

Conversely, programmes and portfolios that are implementing major change may have to temporarily encompass some aspects of business-as-usual in order to minimise the impact on business-as-usual and the organisation's customers.

P3 management has to work closely with operations management to bring about change that becomes routine activity. It is the delivery of these routine products and services that fulfil the strategic mission of the organisation, and it is the expansion or improved effectiveness and efficiency of business-as-usual that usually constitutes the benefits of a project, programme or portfolio.

Further reading
Refer to core texts on pages 4–5.

1.2.3 Strategic management

Definition
Strategic management is the identification, selection and implementation of an organisation's long-term goals and objectives.

General
There are many models for strategic management that generally have three components in common: strategic analysis, strategic choice and strategic implementation.

Strategic analysis starts with the definition of a mission for the organisation. This explains why the organisation exists and provides the context against which strategies will be formulated.

Mission statements usually contain high-level criteria that can be used to evaluate strategies as they are designed and implemented.

All strategic analysis must take account of the organisation's changing external environment (often described using the acronym PESTLE) and its capacity and capability to implement the strategy. Tools commonly used for different aspects of this analysis include the Boston Grid and Ansoff's Matrix.

Strategic choice involves the generation, evaluation and selection of strategic options. Inputs to this process include:

- stakeholders' expectations and aspirations;
- the organisation's strengths;
- the opportunities created by the external environment;
- demands imposed by external influences.

The third stage of strategic management is implementation through projects, programmes and portfolios. The relationship between strategic management and P3 management should be close and symbiotic.

In simple terms, strategic management will set out long-, medium- and short-term goals that are implemented by portfolios, programmes and projects respectively. Successful implementation of strategy depends upon successful P3 management. Together they lead to growth and development of the organisation and the creation of further opportunities and challenges that preface each strategic planning cycle.

In order to judge success, a strategy must have measurable consequences. Tools such as the balanced scorecard help translate strategy into four categories of performance measures: financial, customer, learning and growth, and internal business processes. These provide the basis for defining objectives for projects, programmes and portfolios.

P3 management is therefore of vital importance to strategic management. An organisation should ensure that it establishes governance structures that embed and continuously improve P3 management.

Further reading

Refer to core texts on pages 4–5.

2 People

Projects, programmes and portfolios are ultimately about motivating and coordinating people to achieve specified objectives. In order to do this, an individual manager needs to understand various skills and deliver these in a professional manner. The host organisation needs to promote P3 management as a profession and also provide an environment that encourages individuals to act professionally.

The interpersonal skills section covers those skills that every manager needs but are of prime importance to P3 professionals.

The aim is to describe typical models and processes of human behaviour in each area, not to define what it means to be competent or skilful.

The professionalism section describes aspects of developing and maintaining a professional approach at the individual, organisational and institutional level.

The difference in the application of professionalism at project, programme and portfolio level is one of degree rather than substance. Thus a project manager in a short, stand-alone project has the same responsibility for the learning and development of staff as a portfolio manager overseeing projects and programmes. However, their perspectives will be very different, as will their ability to influence a wider environment. For this reason the professionalism section has no specific project, programme or portfolio dimensions.

2.1 Interpersonal skills

Definition
Interpersonal skills are the means by which people relate to, and interact with, other people.

General
P3 sponsors, managers and team members need to understand and apply interpersonal skills. They must know the limits of their own abilities and ensure that they constantly reassess their strengths and weaknesses and strive for improvement throughout their careers.

Projects, programmes and portfolios are delivered by people. The dynamics, attitudes and relationships between those people are the key enablers to P3 success.

Applying interpersonal skills provides the opportunity to create high-performing teams, build individual effectiveness, develop confidence and drive success. Individuals who actively develop their personal skill set are able to manage their work more successfully.

The ability to communicate is fundamental to all interpersonal skills. A P3 manager uses communications skills to provide leadership to the team, while understanding the dynamics of team development and resolving conflict as it arises.

The P3 manager cannot micro-manage every aspect of the work and must delegate effectively. In a business environment, simple command and control is rarely effective. So the P3 manager must master negotiation and influencing skills to keep the management team and external stakeholders committed to the ultimate objective.

Consistency in the application of behaviour and skills engenders trust and respect. Those people who are acknowledged as having well-developed interpersonal skills are called upon repeatedly to provide advice, guidance, leadership and creativity to resolve challenges and achieve successful outcomes.

The fundamentals of interpersonal skills do not vary across the domains of project, programme and portfolio. However, the context and organisational structures do change and this leads to different challenges and different emphases on the application of the fundamental skills.

Further reading

Hersey, P.H., Blanchard, K.H. and Johnson, D.E., 2012.
Management of organizational behaviour. London: Prentice-Hall.

Stewart, I. and Joines, V., 1987.
TA today: a new introduction to transactional analysis. Chapel Hill, NC: Lifespace.

2.1.1 Communication

Definition

Communication is the means by which information or instructions are exchanged. Successful communication occurs when the received meaning is the same as the transmitted meaning.

General

Communication is fundamental to the P3 environment. Poor communication can lead to misunderstood requirements, unclear goals, alienation of stakeholders, ineffective plans and many other factors that will cause a project, programme or portfolio to fail.

None of the tools and techniques described in this body of knowledge will work without effective communication.

Communication takes many forms. It can be verbal, non-verbal, active, passive, formal, informal, conscious or subconscious. How communication is executed affects understanding and feelings, both of which impact the meaning received.

It must be tailored to convey the communicator's meaning as accurately as possible to the target audience. This is why all projects, programmes and portfolios have a communication management plan that spells out what needs to be communicated: why, how, when and to whom.

There are many factors that affect the effectiveness of communications. Cultural background and transient features, such as mood, current environment and team dynamics, create a 'moving target' for the communicator.

The effective communicator is sensitive to the prevalent atmosphere and structures the message and method of delivery accordingly.

Language should be neutral, clear, objective and avoid unnecessary emotive terms. However, there may be occasions where appropriate emotion and associated delivery mechanisms such as body language can generate a specific, desired effect.

There are often barriers to effective communication. These can be physical, as in the team location or the working environment. They can be cultural, arising perhaps from lack of a common language or understanding across disciplines. Barriers can lead to negative perceptions and related emotions such as envy, fear, mistrust and suspicion.

The range of media available for communication is greater than ever. Paper, telephone and face-to-face meetings are often replaced by email, intranets, social media and SMS messaging.

The wide range of media available provides great opportunity but also increases the risk of poor communication through poor choice of medium.

Selecting an inappropriate delivery medium will create barriers. Poor structure and weak delivery obstruct meaning and have the potential to create barriers to understanding or communication that can hasten or aggravate failure.

Professionals must recognise different needs within their audience and use appropriate and specifically targeted media.

Effective communication is a two-way process. Actively seeking out and listening to feedback are integral parts of good communication. This feedback should inform and make the next round of communication more effective.

Most organisations have well-established communications functions, systems and standards. These should be exploited to the full.

By adhering to organisational standards, projects, programmes and portfolios will be aligned with the organisation as a whole. Such standards may have been developed in relation to specific audiences, both internal and external. Communications with government and regulators often need to follow a particular standard and format.

The importance of tailoring the message and medium to the target audience cannot be overestimated. The communicator must always consider the intended impact of the communication and fashion it accordingly.

Project

A project communication management plan should be prepared as part of the project management plan and is subject to the approval of the sponsor. This is a live document and will be subject to updates as the project progresses and communication requirements change.

A project communication management plan must conform to policies set out in the communication management plans for programmes or portfolios of which the project forms part.

Communication skills will initially be used in gathering stakeholder requirements and preparing a business case. The resulting specifications, plans and governance arrangements must be communicated effectively to obtain approval for the project.

Once it is under way, progress must be communicated and stakeholder support maintained. The project team must understand what is required of them and be confident that appropriate mechanisms are in place to communicate and resolve issues.

All of these factors require the project manager to be a highly competent communicator.

Programme

By their very nature, programmes contain greater uncertainty and complexity than projects. This makes carefully planned communication with the increased range and diversity of stakeholders even more vital.

Programme-level communication will initially focus around the vision. The aim is to ensure that all those affected by the programme have a common understanding of why it is necessary and beneficial.

As more detailed information is developed, the benefits of the programme and how the necessary changes will affect business-as-usual must be communicated.

The levels of change instigated by a programme are often difficult to accept by some groups of stakeholders. Effective communication is central to mitigating the effect of opposition and marshalling support for the programme.

The programme management team must maintain an overview of project communication. Projects will be responsible for their own plans. The programme communication plan must coordinate and harmonise project communications and deal with matters outside the scope of individual projects.

Portfolio

Communication is most effective when it is relevant and targeted. Some communications are better handled at project level, some at programme level and some at portfolio level.

The portfolio management team must establish policies for communication. They must set standards to maintain consistency and determine principles for how each entity within the portfolio will engage with its stakeholders.

Inevitably, there will be overlaps in stakeholder groups. Individuals could find themselves swamped with communications from various projects and programmes. The portfolio must oversee communication across the board without attempting to manage communications on behalf of individual projects and programmes.

Further reading

Collett, P., 2003. *The book of tells, how to read people's minds from their actions*. London: Doubleday.

DeVito, J.A., 2011. *Human communication: the basic course*. 12th ed. Harlow: Allyn and Bacon.

DeVito, J.A., 2012. *The interpersonal communication book*. Boston, MA: Pearson.

Goleman, D., 2007. *Social intelligence: the new science of human relationships*. London: Hutchinson.

2.1.2 Conflict management

Definition
Conflict can be defined as different objectives and attitudes between two or more parties. Conflict management is the process of identifying and addressing differences that, if left unresolved, could affect objectives.

General
The P3 environment is one where many people come together to achieve objectives. There will inevitably be degrees of conflict concerning all aspects of what needs to be done, how it will be done, and who will do it etc.

Not all conflict is negative. Facilitating healthy conflict without suppression can support group development and learning experiences. Conflict is a necessary component of some team development models but, even there, it must be carefully managed to prevent it becoming counterproductive.

Negative interpersonal conflict generally arises from:

- disagreement over a task, objective, decision or action;
- conflicting values;
- unspoken assumptions;
- emotion, including stress, passion, anger, fear, envy and excitement;
- ego, perceived power, influence, and insecurity;
- sense of uncertainty;
- miscommunication.

Whenever negative conflict arises it needs to be tackled before it causes damage. Having clearly defined processes will minimise the negative effects of differences and stop them developing into conflict.

The emergence of conflict can be gradual or sudden. Obvious indications include open hostility, lack of cooperation or direct challenge. Discreet or hidden conflict is more subtly expressed through changes in style or volume of communication, opting out, passive resistance, rumour-mongering or thinly veiled negative remarks.

Unresolved conflict can be expensive. It increases uncertainty, damages morale and undermines long-term team harmony. Ultimately this may lead to failure to deliver objectives and an unhealthy corporate culture.

Resolving conflict is a complex skill but identifying specific techniques or approaches helps to understand what is involved and develop the right competences. There are many models for describing conflict resolution including Blake & Mouton, Thomas-Killman and Pruit.

When addressing conflict it is important to distinguish between the personalities involved, the culture of the organisation and the positions being taken. This can defuse tension and facilitate an objective approach. While facts are readily identifiable, assumptions and emotions are often more difficult to elicit.

In resolving conflict, an appropriate mediator is often required. This can sometimes be necessary where employment issues are concerned and expert knowledge is required.

A mediator must be able to set aside beliefs and values to focus upon the issues. This requires the ability to listen actively, succinctly reflect understanding, and facilitate negotiation towards a resolution.

Typical actions for resolving interpersonal conflict may comprise:

- ensuring an appropriate venue – space, refreshments, accessibility;
- proposing timings, conduct guidance and objectives for each session;
- identifying facts, evidence and assumptions;
- recognising the various levels of stakeholder power and influence;
- assessing the potential impact of personal views;
- agreeing the issues to be resolved, prioritising as required;
- reflecting perspectives, expectations, antagonisms and areas of commonality;
- defining escalation routes if resolution is not possible.

Managing conflict requires sensitivity and empathy, in conjunction with objectivity and an ethical stance.

Project

Conflict can be reduced at the outset of a project through good project planning and communication. The clear definition of scope, time, costs and risks creates a base document, understood by all the stakeholders, which then provides a common starting point for exploring any future conflict.

Clear governance policies enable communication of dissent and improvements in a formal, constructive way. This will include defined escalation procedures, upwards through the programme or portfolio organisation, or to an external function such as HR.

A project manager needs conflict resolution skills but must also know when to ask for help.

Regardless of the approach used to manage or resolve conflict, the project manager must ensure that the outcome is communicated to all those affected.

Programme

The potential for conflict is greater at programme level for several reasons, including the:

- emphasis on implementing business change;
- potential for differing interpretations of the programme vision;
- dependencies between projects within the programme;
- diversity and quantity of stakeholders.

As well as dealing with programme-level conflict, programme management also needs to provide support for project teams who are unable to resolve conflicts at the project level.

Although on a different scale from projects, the nature of conflict within a programme is little different from that in a project.

The main difference is the potential for internal conflict between projects. This may arise, for example, from inputs to one project being outputs from another, or competition over limited resources.

Programme managers need to address conflict through effective planning and control. They must also provide arbitration and clear, timely decision-making.

Portfolio

Interdependencies between projects and programmes within the portfolio will inevitably lead to conflicts over priorities and limited resources. Clear and visible alignment of portfolios to the organisation's strategy will aid resolution of conflicts by justifying and contextualising difficult decisions.

The portfolio manager needs to provide an escalation route for conflict resolution that cannot be resolved within the component programmes or portfolios.

It is also conceivable that some conflict may need to be escalated to the appropriate level within the host organisation. A typical example is industrial relations.

Further reading

Gardiner, P.D., 2005.
Project management, a strategic planning approach. Basingstoke: Palgrave Macmillan.

Stewart, I. and Joines, V., 1987.
TA today: a new introduction to transactional analysis. Chapel Hill, NC: Lifespace.

Ursiny, T., 2003.
The coward's guide to conflict: empowering solutions for those who would rather run than fight. Naperville, IL: Sourcebooks.

2.1.3 Delegation

Definition
Delegation is the practice of giving a person or group the authority to perform the responsibilities of, or act on behalf of, another.

General
While delegation is primarily a mechanism for distributing work, it is also a tool for motivating and training teams and individuals to realise their full potential. Delegation underpins a style of management that encourages project team members to use and develop their skills and knowledge.

The objective of delegation is to get work done by someone else. This is not just a matter of giving instructions on what needs to be done. It also involves matching the work to the behaviour and competences of the delegated resources, as well as giving them the authority to react to situations and make decisions.

The same basic principles and process apply at project, programme and portfolio level. Like leadership, delegation is a mix of process and skill.

In preparation for the delegation process, P3 managers should ensure that they can delegate, are clear that they should delegate, and that time is available to delegate effectively. In doing so they need to recognise that some key functions and activities must remain with them, and that delegation will enable the work to be done better or cheaper by another resource.

The process of delegation is a 'plan, monitor and control' loop and allows the delegator to define:

- what has to be done (clear specification of the work being delegated);
- the control parameters to be maintained (the performance indicators and tolerances that will be applied);
- the monitoring and reporting mechanisms (how progress will be communicated);
- actions to be taken to bring the delegated work back on track should the control parameters be exceeded (escalation and issue management procedures).

Work then needs to be allocated to a team or an individual. Before doing this, the skill of delegation adds four further steps. The P3 manager needs to:

- know the person and their working style;
- agree the level of training or coaching required;
- identify and implement feedback mechanisms;
- identify and implement the reward mechanisms.

Successful delegation is essential to achieve a high-performing team, but there are barriers that prevent it from being done effectively. These include:

- confused lines of authority (in a matrix environment an individual may report to a line manager as well as a project or programme manager);
- availability of appropriately skilled staff (project and programme managers often do not hand pick their team members and have to delegate to people who are not ideally qualified);
- blame culture (if there is intolerance of mistakes, people will be reluctant to accept responsibility);
- excuses by the delegator ('By the time I've explained it, I could have done it myself' is not an acceptable approach).

Project

The structure of a typical project management organisation is based upon implied delegation. While a project sponsor is accountable for the business case, responsibility for its preparation will be implicitly delegated to the project manager or to another role if the project manager has yet to be appointed.

Structured methodologies such as PRINCE2™ make this delegation explicit by spelling out the roles and responsibilities of different members of the project team. If a project is being run without a formal methodology, then the sponsor and project manager must carefully set out a scheme of delegation.

In turn, the project manager may delegate responsibility for packages of work to individuals. This may be a team leader who becomes responsible for delivering certain products, or a specialist who is responsible for managing a particular aspect of the project, e.g. a risk manager or quality manager.

Programme

A programme delegates responsibility for delivering many and varied outputs to its component projects. In many ways delegation encompasses the essence of programme management: the focus on managing delegated work.

A programme delegates the creation of outputs to projects and the realisation of benefits to change management teams. It then monitors the work of both groups. It is the responsibility of the programme management team to define the monitoring and reporting mechanisms, specify tolerances and provide support to resolve escalated issues.

Project management teams should be permitted to manage within their remit, while the programme management team concentrate on the interdependencies between projects and any work that lies outside the scope of individual projects.

Portfolio

A portfolio is designed to achieve strategic objectives. The ways in which these strategic objectives may be achieved has to respond to changing external influences. This raises the likelihood that the work delegated by the portfolio management team to the individual programmes and projects may be subject to large-scale change.

As the scale of the delegated work increases, so does its susceptibility to change driven by external factors. The portfolio management team must therefore be adept at revisiting the specification of delegated work, adjusting priorities and rebalancing resources whilst retaining a robust culture of delegation and escalation.

Further reading

Goleman, D., Boyatzis, R. and McKee, A., 2002.
Primal leadership. Boston, MA: Harvard Business School Press.

2.1.4 Influencing

Definition
Influencing is the act of affecting the behaviours and actions of others.

General
P3 managers can rarely achieve their objectives through direct authority alone, so their ability to influence others is a core skill. Even in those instances where authority can be exercised, it is better to temper it through influence. In this way, actions and behaviours become willing rather than simply obedient.

Successful intervention can be measured though changes in attitude, behaviour and decision-making that reflect the aim of the influencer. Success can also be seen through acceptance, support and agreement to the influencer's proposals or objectives.

In order to be effective in influencing others, individuals or groups need to be able to assess and understand their own patterns of attitude, behaviour, emotion and decision-making.

Such patterns will be formed from a complex range of experiences, cultural aspects, contextual situations and emotional states. Influencing, at all levels, is inextricably linked with negotiation, conflict management, leadership, communications and teamwork.

Effective influence requires:

- sensory awareness (understanding your own behaviour and that of others);
- emotional intelligence (representing your own feelings and those of others);
- communication skills (flexibility in approaches, methods and media);
- negotiation skills (ability to persuade and find a mutually acceptable position);
- contextual awareness (ability to select the appropriate time, place and contributors);
- cultural awareness (understanding the wide diversity of factors, from background, race, gender and learning styles, to communication, values and beliefs).

Influencing can be overt, discreet, conscious or subconscious and can be applied to any, or all, stakeholders. The actions of an individual or group can also indirectly influence others who are not stakeholders. For example, a team working on a new product or service may be very positive about their task. This enthusiasm then becomes general knowledge and leads others in the wider organisation to ask about the work and even to seek to participate in it or use its products.

An individual's influence is demonstrated through their behaviour. It can be related to job title, position in the organisation and perceptions of power and control, but does not have to be.

Influence evolves as relationships are built between parties. Relationships can be based on positive factors such as shared values, ethical positions, trust and genuine liking and respect. In some situations influencing is wholly based on perceived authority. This can be negative as it provides an ability to influence based upon fear and insecurity. This, in turn, can easily become a form of control that leads to compliance without commitment.

Project

A project manager has nominal authority over the members of a project team. However, in a matrix environment team members may also report to line managers who are responsible for their conditions of employment.

In leading the team, the project manager cannot rely on authority alone. Influencing skills will be required with individual team members and also with their line managers in the case of conflicting demands.

The relationship between the project manager and the project sponsor is central to the success of a project. The two roles have different perspectives on the project so they will use influencing skills with each other to develop a common approach to the project.

The most obvious target for pure application of influencing techniques is with project stakeholders who are not part of the project team and not subject to the project manager's authority. Some will be supportive and others will be antagonistic.

The project manager will use influencing and communication skills to encourage active support from some stakeholders and mitigate the objections of others.

Programme

The programme manager employs similar influencing skills but has to temper these efforts based upon the level of interaction they are able to achieve with their project managers and stakeholders. Given the more strategic nature of programme management, the ability to influence can be more dependent upon job title and the reputation of the individuals involved.

The range of stakeholders that need to be influenced on a programme is large. A programme manager needs to ensure that stakeholders are engaged at the appropriate level.

Whilst a particular stakeholder may only be concerned with one project, the relevant project manager may be of insufficient status to exert the necessary influence. Where a stakeholder is affected by multiple projects, it may be best for influence to be applied at programme level to ensure that different projects do not attempt to influence in different directions.

A defining aspect of programmes is that they implement organisational change and impact the operation of business-as-usual activity. This is an area where the use of influencing skills is important.

Organisations cannot be effectively changed through authority alone. Influencing is a primary skill in establishing change that is durable and long lasting. Programmes will have business change managers, who will be responsible for influencing the many stakeholders who need to actively embrace change in order to achieve the required benefits.

Portfolio

The strategic nature of portfolio management inevitably requires the involvement and support of executive teams and management boards throughout the organisation.

They must establish corporate visibility and create the right environment to enable the benefits from portfolio management to be realised across the business. Strong influencing skills will be required to facilitate decision-making and action in all phases of the portfolio life cycle.

A portfolio is the most visible aspect of P3 management to the outside world. If the host organisation wishes to influence shareholders, public opinion, customers, etc., then ownership and commitment to the portfolio are required at the highest level.

Further reading

Cialdini, R.B., 2008.
Influence: science and practice. 5th ed. London: Pearson.

Dent, F.E. and Brent, M., 2006.
Influencing, skills and techniques for business success. London: Palgrave Macmillan.

2.1.5 Leadership

Definition
Leadership is the ability to establish vision and direction, to influence and align others towards a common purpose, and to empower and inspire people to achieve success.

General
There are many theories of leadership and the subject can be approached in a variety of ways. One simple approach to understanding different leadership styles is the comparison of transactional leaders and transformational leaders.

Transactional leaders ensure that requirements are agreed and that the rewards and penalties for achievement, or lack of it, are understood. It is an exchange process to do with setting objectives and plans: 'do this and you will be rewarded thus'.

In contrast, transformational leaders do everything possible to help people succeed in their own right and become leaders themselves. They help those people to transform themselves and achieve more than was intended or even thought possible.

By definition, the P3 environment is one of change. New teams come together to achieve objectives and are disbanded when the work is complete. As a consequence, the P3 manager should focus on different aspects of leadership throughout the P3 life cycle and set the pace accordingly.

Early phases require expertise in influencing stakeholders and creating vision but may need a more transactional style with the P3 team. As the work progresses, the leadership focus shifts to maintaining momentum, responding to change and applying a more transformational approach.

The position of leader is granted by followers who make the decision to follow. That decision will be influenced by the leader using an appropriate style of leadership that takes account of both the situation and the readiness of people to follow.

Team members' willingness to follow will vary according to their levels of motivation and ability, as well as their loyalties, priorities and the context of the situation.

Leaders must be aware of their team members' motivational requirements in order to manage their approach to individuals flexibly. The motivation of individuals is the subject of many theoretical models, such as those proposed by Maslow, Herzberg and McGregor.

A leader provides constructive and immediate feedback on the performance of individuals and encourages feedback on their own performance. To enable continual improvement, lessons learned will be shared and success celebrated. Leaders can act as a coach and/or mentor to team members to promote personal growth and development.

They should be aware of how their authority will be perceived by stakeholders at different phases of the life cycle. The authority required may be based on expert knowledge, or may originate from other forms of influence such as gaining trust, confidence, inspiration and the development of teamwork.

Leaders must adapt their approach according to the needs of those being led. This is called situational leadership and is explained in models such as Hersey and Blanchard's Leadership Model and Blake and Mouton's management grid.

Leadership should be exercised at all levels within projects, programmes and portfolios and can be exercised by all or some of the team. For instance, team members will provide leadership to their colleagues and this has a positive impact on the organisation.

Project

The role of leadership in a project is to promote the project objectives, encourage positive relationships, support effective teamwork, raise morale, and empower and inspire individuals.

Leaders require followers, but leaders must also themselves be able to follow. Many projects will be part of a programme or portfolio that also has its leader. A project manager will need to be a strong leader but must also be able to be an effective team member in respect of the programme or portfolio.

Most projects will use resources from the host organisation. These team members will come from functional departments which have their own managers who also provide leadership. The environment where individuals are simultaneously part of a project team and a functional team is called matrix management. The project manager's approach to leadership must acknowledge that those being led also have functional duties and loyalties.

A pragmatic project manager must balance the theories of leadership with the practical need to deliver the project objectives and the limits on their authority to lead.

Programme

The nature of a programme influences the required leadership style of the programme manager:

- the objectives of a programme are visionary and more fluid than a project;
- many of the people who need to be led are themselves leaders;
- programmes implement change and affect a wide range of stakeholders.

A vision is more difficult to communicate than a set of product specifications. A programme manager is less likely to gain credibility and authority through technical expertise than through visionary leadership that is visible to all programme and project team members.

The programme manager needs to develop strong leadership skills to establish credibility with a team of committed leaders in their own right. This is especially true where actions that best serve the programme are in conflict with what a project manager believes are in the best interests of the project or a business change manager believes are not in the best interests of business-as-usual.

The fact that a programme implements change means that some of those directly affected by the programme will be affected in ways that they do not see as personally beneficial. Leadership will be needed to champion the organisational benefits of the programme and influence others to accept, if not actively support, the necessary change.

Portfolio

Portfolio leadership is the most visionary in nature as the single purpose of the portfolio is to deliver the host organisation's strategy.

Leadership must ensure that there is a mechanism for prioritisation and balancing of resources. It must maintain clear decision-making and accountability. Above all, the commitment of senior management to the changes implemented by the portfolio will clearly reflect good leadership.

The portfolio manager will reinforce the strategy through other leaders who are involved in the portfolio. Strong leadership at the portfolio level will set the scene for leadership throughout the component programmes, projects and relevant areas of business-as-usual.

Further reading

Goleman, D., Boyatzis, R. and McKee, A., 2002.
Primal leadership. Boston, MA: Harvard Business School Press.

Lewis, J.P., 2003.
Project leadership. London: McGraw-Hill.

2.1.6 Negotiation

Definition
Negotiation is a discussion between two or more parties aimed at reaching agreement.

General
Negotiations can take place at any time in a project, programme or portfolio and may be formal or informal in nature.

Formal negotiations are typically with providers on such issues as agreeing contracts. Informal negotiations include discussions to resolve conflict, or discussions to obtain internal resources.

Negotiation skills are used in many areas of P3 management such as conflict management, contract management, requirements management and stakeholder management. Good negotiation skills include:

- an ability to set goals and limits;
- emotional control;
- excellent listening skills;
- excellent verbal communication skills;
- knowledge of when and how to close the negotiation.

Negotiation falls within two categories:

- competitive negotiation;
- collaborative negotiation.

Competitive negotiation implies getting the best deal regardless of the needs and interests of the other party. This form of negotiation can easily become a battle where the winner takes all. While competitive negotiation should be avoided, it may not always be possible.

Collaborative negotiation seeks to create a 'win-win' scenario where all parties involved get part or all of what they were looking for from the negotiation. This approach tends to produce the best results, helps build long-term relationships and minimises the opportunity for conflict.

The process of negotiation can be divided into a number of distinct phases:

- planning: Prepare by gathering as much information as possible. Set goals and ensure that they accord with the tolerances which have been agreed. Investigate relevant social conventions if planning to negotiate with people from different cultures. Clarify the escalation route to use in the event of being unable to resolve the negotiation;
- discussing: P3 managers are often, but not always, required to open the negotiations by setting the scene, then explore and discuss the key issues. They must listen, probe and question, paraphrase regularly and check understanding;
- proposing: Make a proposal. Communicate clearly and openly;
- bargaining: Be prepared for trade-offs;
- agreement: There is no substitute for a written record;
- review: On resolution, the outcome needs to be communicated to all parties and the consequences incorporated within the P3 management plan.

Some of the common pitfalls associated with negotiations include:

- being ill-prepared;
- opening negotiations with an unreasonable offer;
- not taking 'time-outs' when the negotiations are unduly protracted;
- rushing negotiations in order to secure a quick agreement;
- failing to walk away if an agreement is not possible without breaching tolerances;
- not remaining calm.

Project

Project managers need to apply negotiation skills throughout the project life cycle. Early on in a project, as requirements are being captured and initial plans produced, the project manager may need to balance the time, cost, quality and scope requirements of the project and negotiate with stakeholders.

As resources are mobilised or procured, the project manager will need to negotiate internally with line managers who 'own' the resources and conduct more formal contract negotiations with potential providers.

As the project progresses, conflicts will arise. The project manager will need to negotiate solutions to conflicts, whether they are informal or contractual.

In some environments, there may be specialist support available. It is important for project managers to know when to ask for help from, for example, the HR or legal departments within the host organisation.

Programme

The range of negotiation scenarios within a programme will be broad. The programme manager must understand when to allow negotiations to be handled at project level and when to take responsibility at programme level.

A balance must be struck between removing autonomy from project managers and gaining an advantage by collectively negotiating on behalf of the programme as a whole.

A programme includes project outputs that impose change on business-as-usual. This will inevitably cause situations where a negotiated solution is needed.

A programme is more likely to have access to specialist negotiators, but programme managers should still be skilled negotiators in their own right. Programme managers and programme sponsors are the visible leadership of the programme and may need to become personally involved to achieve a successful conclusion.

Portfolio

A portfolio will encompass the broadest range of negotiation scenarios and will need access to various specialists to negotiate HR, legal and internal issues. The only escalation from the portfolio is to the organisation's managing board that must be fully committed to the portfolio's strategic objectives and supportive in negotiations.

Further reading

Fisher, R. and Shapiro, D., 2007.
Building agreement: using emotions as you negotiate. London: Random House.

Fisher, R., Ury, W. and Patton, B., 2003.
Getting to yes: negotiating an agreement without giving in. London: Random House.

74   **APM Body of Knowledge** 6th edition

2.1.7 Teamwork

Definition
Teamwork is a group of people working in collaboration or by cooperation towards a common goal.

General
A team consists of a group of people, committed to a common goal that no one individual can achieve alone. The focus of teams and teamwork is on mutual accountability and performance.

The concept of teamwork presents itself differently across the projects, programmes and portfolios as the make-up and environment of the teams vary. Within the P3 environment there will be a hierarchy of different teams. The obvious example is a project team within a programme, a programme team within a portfolio and the overall portfolio team.

Regardless of whether they are involved in team selection, P3 managers should consider a number of factors when developing a team. Individuals will have different skills and personalities. They may come from different cultures and working environments. The team may be physically co-located or work virtually across different time zones. The impact of all these factors on teamworking needs to be considered.

The establishment of a team will initially involve the selection of individuals based on their skills, behaviours and attitudes. Teamworking is most effective when people with complementary skills and behaviours are committed to a common objective and method of working.

Models such as Belbin and Margerison-McCann illustrate how different personalities work together to create a working team. Each personality has its strengths and weaknesses. Within the team, one person's strengths balance another's weaknesses. Individuals will perform better in a team context if they are given a role that plays to their strengths.

The use of psychometric tools, such as the Myers-Briggs Type Inventory, may also help the P3 manager and team members understand and value the differences between individuals.

Once assembled, teams do not simply become high-performing because they have been given a common objective. They go through a series of development stages as illustrated by Tuckman or Katzenbach & Smith. The P3 manager must be aware of where a team is in the development cycle and adjust the leadership style to suit.

Projects, programmes and portfolios evolve throughout their life-cycle phases. This changing environment will alter the balance and dynamics of a team. Effective teamworking is a valuable commodity and needs constant nurturing by the P3 manager.

Teamwork may be within a tightly integrated team or in a collaborative working group.

In integrated teams, the emphasis is on the team developing together as a unit and working jointly on objectives. Collaborative groups share information, insights and perspectives, supporting each other to do their job better, but the focus is on each individual's performance and accountability.

Project

The project environment is where the most close-knit teams will be found. The nature of a traditional project is that the ultimate deliverable is well defined and often broken down into a series of well-specified products. This provides the focus for the team's efforts.

The project manager must communicate details of the project deliverable to the team and how it will be achieved. All team members must be committed to the end product and understand their role in its development.

On larger projects, the project manager may delegate the development of component products to team managers. By implication, the project manager is delegating responsibility for team development as well, but must retain an overview of performance.

The project manager is responsible for the continued cohesion of the team and should strive to keep individuals motivated and support them in their personal and career development aspirations.

While a common focus on a well-defined goal is an important tool for developing a team, it can also be a weakness. All projects are susceptible to change. Sometimes this is due to unavoidable external factors, but often it will be due to changing requirements from stakeholders. If the team is focused on a well-defined goal, constant change can be demotivating.

In environments where change is frequent, or requirements need to be flexible, project managers may choose an Agile approach. This develops a team with a different mindset as teams are often self-organising and may use techniques such as 'timeboxing' and 'sprint planning'.

Programme

Within a programme there will be a number of sub-teams that the programme manager needs to develop as well as the overall 'team'. These could include, for example, the:

■ team of project managers;
■ team of business change managers;
■ support team (risk manager, communications manager, administrators, etc.).

These sub-teams will be developed concurrently with the objective of achieving the programme's vision and component benefits. The levels of responsibility of the team members may mean that a collaborative working group approach is more relevant. While individual managers will take responsibility for the development of their own teams, the programme manager must create an overall team ethos for the programme as a whole.

Inevitably there will be a significant turnover rate within the programme team as projects are instigated and closed or as business-as-usual units go through the change management process.

Maintaining a team ethos across this broad, diverse and changing community will require excellent communication and leadership skills on the part of the programme manager.

Portfolio

The concept of teamworking will not be as visible in the portfolio dimension. The intensity of human interaction associated with integrated teamworking is not present, other than in the core portfolio management team. The wider group of individuals with responsibility to deliver different parts of the portfolio form a collaborative team.

It is in the interest of the portfolio manager that the appropriate type of teamworking is encouraged and exploited at all levels to maximise portfolio performance. Collaborative and cooperative working within the portfolio with a shared vision of the strategic objectives should also be encouraged.

Further reading

Katzenbach, J.R. and Smith, D.K., 2005.
The wisdom of teams. New York, NY: Harper Business.

Margerison, C. and McKann, D., 1995.
Team management: practical new approaches. 2nd ed. Didcot: Management Books 2000.

2.2 **Professionalism**

Definition

Professionalism is the application of expert and specialised knowledge within a specific field and the acceptance of standards relating to that profession.

General

All professions have similar features. They can be summarised as follows:

- a profession creates and owns a distinctive, relevant body of knowledge;
- members of the profession need to attain a level of skill and continue to practise and apply themselves to on-going learning in order to maintain appropriate skills;
- individual members should follow a code of professional ethical conduct and behave in an appropriate manner;
- members of the profession should seek to act in the public interest;
- a profession should award certificates to practice, based on examination of individuals' competence.

Responsibility for developing and maintaining a profession occurs at three levels: institutional, organisational and individual. In P3 management, at the institutional level, APM has a framework with five dimensions:

- breadth – the scope of P3 management as defined by the *APM Body of Knowledge*;
- depth – the skills and behaviours required as defined by the *APM Competence Framework*;
- achievement – the provision of APM qualifications;
- commitment – CPD throughout a career;
- accountability – adherence to the *APM Code of Professional Conduct*.

The publications, qualifications and activities of APM are all designed to support the APM 5 Dimensions of Professionalism.

At the organisational level, companies, government departments and other types of organisations need to provide support and governance for all those involved in projects, programmes and portfolios. This will include well-defined career paths, education programmes and communities of practice.

At an individual level, those working as professionals on projects, programmes and portfolios need to take responsibility for their own development and behaviour.

This includes education and training to develop knowledge and promote competence, professional behaviour to promote trust, and continuing professional development to demonstrate commitment.

Further reading

Association for Project Management, 2011.
APM *code of professional conduct.*
[online] Available at: www.apm.org.uk/ProfessionalConduct.asp [Accessed 23 August 2011].

2.2.1 Communities of practice

Definition
Communities of practice are groups of people who share a concern or passion for an aspect of P3 management and develop expertise through regular interaction.

General
P3 professionals are often spread throughout an organisation and rarely form separate departments or functional areas. This combined with the continual movement of project and programme staff from team to team and location to location, means that those involved in projects and programmes are less able to learn from shared experience.

Establishing a community of practice (CoP) enables P3 professionals to be part of a virtual department that shares experiences and contributes to improving future practice.

The three characteristics that are critical to a CoP are:

1. the domain: The CoP has an identity defined by a shared domain of interest. It may be very broad (e.g. P3 management) or more specific (e.g. project control). Membership implies a commitment to the domain. The members value their collective competence and learn from each other;
2. the community: In pursuing their interest in their domain, members engage in joint activities and discussions, help each other, and share information. They build relationships that enable them to learn from each other;
3. the practice: Members of a community of practice develop a shared repertoire of resources – experiences, stories, tools (e.g. tools for risk management, knowledge management, scheduling, etc.) and ways of addressing recurring problems.

There are a number of benefits to a CoP. It:

- provides a home for the profession by allowing potentially isolated people to come together;
- assists in the dissemination of knowledge (e.g. new practices, lessons learned);
- motivates its members, as they feel part of a community of like-minded people, rather than part of a team from different disciplines;
- provides mutual support and encouragement between members of the community and an opportunity to test ideas;

- helps generate new knowledge (e.g. from the formation of special interest groups);
- helps accelerate an organisation through its maturity journey by sharing best practice.

Communities of practice can take many different forms. They should be constituted according to the needs of the organisation.

Some CoPs relate solely to an organisation, while others are sector-based, such as the Pharmaceutical Industry Project Management Group (PIPMG). The APM's own specific interest groups (SIGs) are examples of communities of practice that focus on particular aspects of P3 management.

Some corporate CoPs are formally constituted and 'own' the profession and discipline of P3 management within their parent organisation. They may be responsible for professionalism and take responsibility for learning and development, knowledge management and maturity development. Others are simply informal communities of people who want to share experience.

In order to make a difference, communities of practice need to be actively supported. Regular meetings, social media groups and events promote knowledge sharing and embed the sense of professionalism.

Further reading

McDermott, R. and Archibald, D., 2010.
Harnessing your staff's informal networks, Harvard Business Review, March 2010, [online] Available at: www.apm.org.uk/BoK6FurtherReading.

McDermott, R. and Archibald, D., 2010.
Harnessing your staff's informal networks, Harvard Business Review, March 2010.

Overseas Development Institute, 2009.
Communities of practice: linking knowledge, policy and practice.
[online] Available at: www.apm.org.uk/BoK6FurtherReading.

Wenger, E., (2006.
Communities of practice: a brief introduction.
[online] Available at: www.apm.org.uk/BoK6FurtherReading.

Wenger, E., McDermott, R. and Snyder, W., 2002.
Cultivating communities of practice: a guide to managing knowledge. Boston, MA: Harvard Business School Press.

2.2.2 Competence

Definition
Competence is the combined knowledge, skill and behaviour that a person needs to perform properly in a job or work role.

General
Within competence, knowledge is the theoretical understanding of a subject, skills are the practical manifestation of knowledge, and behaviour represents the personal attributes that control how an individual applies their knowledge and skill.

Competence and competency are widely used terms with many different interpretations. The terms are frequently used interchangeably, though the distinction can be made between a competency as a personal attribute of an individual and a competence as a statement of standards that can be demonstrated by performance and outputs.

Competences are commonly broken down further into technical and behavioural competencies. A technical competency may, for example, be the ability to use a particular scheduling technique (e.g. 'able to perform critical path analysis'). A behavioural competency indicates how someone acts in specific circumstances (e.g. 'actively seeks schedule estimates from team members').

Many organisations develop competence frameworks with a view to managing recruitment and professional development more effectively. Such frameworks provide a structure which defines the individual competencies required by people working with that organisation, or part of the organisation.

In the P3 domain, such a framework should identify competencies for all aspects of P3 management which can then be used flexibly to build role descriptions to suit differing contexts and circumstances.

The P3 manager can use a competence framework when forming a management team to define roles and then use competency-based interviewing techniques to identify the best person for each role.

Only the P3 manager can make decisions about how to utilise the range of human resources available. The value of competences and competence frameworks is that they provide an objective tool that helps define expectations for team and individual capability and performance.

Competences and competence frameworks should reflect the needs of the work, including those of stakeholders and sponsors, as well as those directly working on projects, programmes or portfolios.

An ill-fitting, or not clearly specified, competence approach serves to hinder rather than help. At their best, competences and competence frameworks provide a clear set of well-defined statements about expected performance and outcomes. This can lead to fairer and more transparent appraisal systems, and give a clear link between individual performance and project performance. When designed or used inappropriately, they can be difficult to use, result in the expectation that everyone should behave in the same way, and fail to deliver on improvements in performance.

Where an organisation wants to raise the overall capability of its workforce, it can use competency assessment to identify strengths and weaknesses at an organisational or individual level. Such information is invaluable in establishing learning and development programmes.

Competence frameworks can be designed in a number of ways. Some organisations develop their own bespoke framework, while others use existing external competence frameworks, in whole or in part. Regardless of how they are developed, competence frameworks are a key component of learning and development for individuals, and for developing the maturity of the organisation.

Further reading

Chartered Institute of Personnel and Development, 2011.
Competence and competency frameworks.
[online] Available at: www.apm.org.uk/BoK6FurtherReading.

Franklin, M., 2010.
Building project management capability through competency assessments.
[online] Available at: www.apm.org.uk/BoK6FurtherReading.

International Project Management Association, 2006.
ICB-IPMA competence baseline. 3rd ed.
[online] Available at: www.apm.org.uk/BoK6FurtherReading.

Spencer, L.M. and Spencer, S.M., 1993.
Competence at work: models for superior performance. Chichester: Wiley.

2.2.3 Ethics frameworks

Definition
An ethics framework sets recognised standards of conduct and behaviour within the P3 profession.

General
A key requirement of a profession is that individual members should act ethically.

Trust and respect are vital to the success of anyone who wants to be regarded as a professional. This trust is gained by working consistently in a moral, legal and socially appropriate manner. It is reinforced by a commitment to act in accordance with a code of conduct.

Ethical leadership depends on a fundamental understanding of the legal boundaries (such as the UK Bribery Act) and stakeholders' norms of behaviour, expectations and moral values. The latter will vary by location, culture and sector.

The P3 manager needs to consider the ethics of the process by which deliverables are produced and the use to which they are to be (or could be) put. A basic knowledge of ethical theory and how to resolve ethical dilemmas is needed in order to deal with these issues.

The moral values of different stakeholders, as well as the relevant national and international laws, have to be understood.

Personal and professional codes of conduct do not always align with those of the organisations involved in projects, programmes and portfolios and this can lead to conflict. The P3 manager must ensure that the project, programme or portfolio's values, or code of conduct, are clearly articulated and understood by all. This can be achieved through training, taking part in workshops or issuing specific guidance.

The most powerful way to ensure that teams and stakeholders understand and abide by the code is for the P3 manager to lead by example.

If a professional believes that they have a conflict of interest, or difficulties with the ethics of their activities, then advice or direction should be sought from a relevant authority.

Society now demands increasing transparency and expects professionals to behave in an ethical manner. So the P3 manager needs to be able to take and explain ethical decisions in a way that maintains the commitment of all stakeholders.

Further reading

Crane, A. and Matten, D., 2010.
Business ethics: managing corporate citizenship and sustainability in the age of globalization. 3rd ed. Oxford: Oxford University Press.

Trevino, L. and Nelson, K., 2010.
Managing business ethics: straight talk about how to do it right. 5th ed. Wiley: Chichester.

2 People

2.2.4 Learning and development

Definition
Learning and development encompass the continual improvement of competence at all levels of an organisation.

General
Within an organisation, learning and development needs are set by performance management. This determines the relationship between people's ability levels and the expectation of the organisation. Identification, application and monitoring of learning within projects, programmes and portfolios develops the organisation's delivery capability.

The gap between expectation and ability is normally addressed by planned learning and development programmes. These might involve a short-term response, e.g. a one-day course, or a long-term approach, e.g. a three-year, part-time MSc.

The skills that need to be developed might be specifically job related, as in the use of a software tool or a management process, or aimed at a specific project, programme or portfolio-related qualification. In the P3 environment, learning and development also often take the form of courses that lead to professional qualifications such as APMP or PRINCE2™ Practitioner.

Organisations vary widely in their ability to deliver learning and development. The 'blue-chip' approach may involve the creation of an 'academy' or 'university' offering a wealth of courses and qualifications. A small organisation, however, will rely more on internal support and mentoring and provision by external providers.

The scope and timescale of individual work commitments will directly affect the nature of learning and the type of development activity. Most organisations will use a variety of approaches, selecting the right approach for their needs and those of their staff.

P3 managers have a role in providing an environment that supports the learning and development of staff. Individually, they will also be involved in performance reviews and suggestions for future career development.

P3-based organisations and their managers realise the need to have a well-educated and skilled workforce. However, this does not mean that individuals can abrogate responsibility for their own continuing professional development (CPD). An organisation's performance management system will typically encourage individuals and their supervisors to identify gaps in knowledge and skills.

88   **APM Body of Knowledge** 6th edition

Individuals may be part of a project, programme or portfolio for several years and their welfare needs to be managed accordingly. This requires appropriate staff induction, career development plans, skills needs analysis, and development and training.

Organisations need to recognise that CPD for staff remains an overarching principle. P3 managers must recognise the need for individuals to undertake CPD to keep pace with changing standards, legislation, tools, techniques and methods.

CPD in its most basic form involves:

■ identifying current and future needs;
■ setting specific learning objectives;
■ planning activities to support development;
■ recording activities and achievements.

Professional bodies play an important role by maintaining records of attendance and dossiers of CPD certificates for their members. APM's own CPD scheme can be used to both structure personal development plans and highlight an individual's commitment to the profession.

The learning and development needs of organisations, teams and individuals are in a constant state of flux as they attempt to meet the challenges and competitive forces of the marketplace. This requires a dynamic approach to learning and development, using all the tools available.

Further reading

Refer to core texts on pages 4–5.

3 Delivery

This area is about the delivery of outputs, outcomes and benefits. Six of the sections deal with the fundamental components of every project, programme and portfolio:

- Scope: what are the objectives and scope of the work?
- Schedule: how long will it take to achieve?
- Finance: how are necessary funds acquired and costs managed?
- Risk: what are the threats and opportunities involved?
- Quality: how will fitness for purpose of the deliverables and management processes be assured?
- Resource: how will the necessary resources be acquired, mobilised and managed?

Some aspects of P3 delivery do not fit neatly into these fundamentals. They are process-based topics (e.g. planning) or integrative topics (e.g. business case). These are collected together under the general title of management and have relationships with all the other six sections.

3.1 Integrative management

Definition
The application of management processes that integrate some or all fundamental components of scope, schedule, cost, risk, quality and resources.

General
The topics in this section do not directly address the fundamental components of scope, schedule, cost, risk, quality and resources. They are integrative topics that bring together some or all of the components and comprise:

- business case;
- control;
- information management;
- organisation;
- planning;
- stakeholder management.

The planning process has two functions. Firstly, it sets out the policies for managing the fundamental components. Secondly, it defines and estimates what needs to be done; how it should be done; and when it should be done.

Control processes take the outputs of the planning process as a baseline and track what actually happens against what was planned to happen. Control methods are normally focused on dealing with deviations from plan and attempting to return to plan. However, control also involves assessing whether to terminate work that is no longer viable.

The planning and control processes create a large amount of information covering the content and governance of the work. This information needs to be created, updated and communicated effectively for planning and controlling the work.

The business case is the key document for projects and programmes. It states why they are worth the investment. Preparing a business case requires the summarisation and integration of information from all the components.

There are many people involved in a project, programme or portfolio. Some are directly involved in managing or performing the work, while others are simply affected by the work. Some have influence and others do not. The organisation topic describes the management team and its roles and responsibilities.

The stakeholder management topic explains how people who are involved in, or affected by, the work in any way must be identified and engaged.

Further reading

Refer to core texts on pages 4–5.

3.1.1 Business case

Definition

The business case provides justification for undertaking a project or programme. It evaluates the benefit, cost and risk of alternative options and provides a rationale for the preferred solution.

General

All projects and programmes must have a business case that demonstrates the value of the work.

In the concept phase of the life cycle an outline business case is prepared that is then used by senior management to assess whether to give the go-ahead for the definition phase. The detailed business case is prepared during the latter phase.

The project or programme is owned by the sponsor, who has ultimate accountability for ensuring that the benefits are achieved. However, the project or programme manager will usually be responsible for preparing the business case, possibly with specialist support.

Once approved, the business case must be kept up to date, reflecting approved changes. In this way, it can be used as the primary document at gate reviews to determine if the work should continue.

A business case typically includes the:

- strategic case – the background of the project or programme and why it is needed;
- options appraisal – what options have been considered and which has been chosen (not forgetting the 'do nothing' option);
- expected benefits – the benefits that will arise from the work and any unavoidable disbenefits;
- commercial aspects – the costs, investment appraisal and funding arrangements;
- risk – the major risks and their impact on the business case;
- timescales – a summary of the delivery of outputs and realisation of benefits.

Project

The content of the business case should be adapted to reflect the specific project requirements and context. For example:

- if a contracting organisation is delivering a project for a client organisation, the contractor's business case will be based around the profitability of delivering the project output. The client's business case will be based around the benefits derived from the output;

- where a project is stand-alone, the project management team will have to develop their own business case. Where a project is part of a programme, it will usually have its business case provided by the programme management team;
- for large projects it is reasonable to assume that a larger degree of risk is involved than with smaller projects. Therefore, the sponsor and other members of senior management will require a greater level of detail within the business case to give them confidence.

Programme

A programme business case must accommodate the greater uncertainty that exists in a programme environment. Whenever possible, it should provide justification for the programme based on quantifiable benefits, rather than broad assumptions of value.

Programmes are usually broken down into tranches. It can be useful to have a business case for each tranche. This ensures that, if the programme is terminated at the end of a tranche, those that have already been completed will have delivered some beneficial change.

Programmes must monitor the interdependencies between projects and ensure that problems affecting one project that affect the business case of another, are identified and communicated. Similarly, the programme management team must ensure that factors occurring in business-as-usual are identified and communicated.

Portfolio

Since a portfolio is not a stand-alone enterprise, but rather a collection of programmes, projects and business-as-usual elements, the portfolio does not require its own business case. The programmes and projects within it each have their own.

The business cases of the projects and programmes in the portfolio will be derived from the strategic objectives that the portfolio is designed to achieve. The portfolio management team will then use the business cases to categorise, prioritise and balance the portfolio.

Further reading

Buttrick, R., 2010.
The project workout: the ultimate handbook of project and programme management. 4th ed. Harlow: FT Prentice-Hall.

HM Treasury, 2003.
The green book. [online] Available at: www.apm.org.uk/BoK6FurtherReading.

Rogers, M., 2001.
Engineering project appraisal. Oxford: Blackwell Science.

3.1.2 Control

Definition
Control comprises tracking performance against agreed plans and taking the corrective action required to meet defined objectives.

General
All six fundamental components of delivery need to be controlled. Some techniques, such as change control and quality control, are specific to one of the elements. Others, such as earned value management, bring together multiple elements. Fundamentally, all techniques fall into three broad categories.

Cybernetic control (from the Greek for helmsman) deals with routine progress tracking and corrective action. This is the central role of the P3 manager.

In order to track progress, there must be a baseline against which to compare it. It is the manager's responsibility to steer the work so that progress remains as close to the baseline as possible. To do this effectively, the manager must have agreed tolerances within which the work can be managed.

Tolerances are acceptable deviations from the baseline plan. If performance is outside, or predicted to be outside, the agreed tolerances, this is classed as an 'issue' that must be escalated to the sponsor. The sponsor and manager will then agree on the appropriate corrective action. If the result is a major change to the work, then a new baseline may be agreed against which future performance is tracked.

A common method of illustrating performance is 'RAG reporting' (Red, Amber, Green). Green status means performance is within tolerances and predicted to remain there. Amber is within tolerances but predicted to exceed them. Red indicates performance has exceeded tolerances.

Go/no go control deals with the key decision points that are built into the life cycle. These are typically found at the end of a phase, stage or tranche of work and involve a major review of what has been delivered.

At these decision points, the sponsor considers the available information and decides whether to proceed with the remaining work. In extreme cases a project, programme, or even portfolio, may be terminated because it is no longer viable.

Post-control is entirely backward-looking. It is concerned with learning from experience through, for example, post-project or post-programme reviews.

The success of a project, programme or portfolio and the maturity of the organisation are both highly dependent upon the ability to establish and act upon lessons learned.

Another way of looking at control techniques is to see them as either event-driven or time-driven.

Go/no go and post-control techniques are always event-driven. They are triggered, for example, by the end of a stage, or the end of a programme. An important event-driven control is the one triggered by progress that exceeds tolerances.

Time-driven techniques are more applicable to cybernetic control and involve weekly or monthly reports, periodic reviews or regular progress meetings. It is the manager's job to collect progress data and prepare regular reports showing the performance of the work for all of the elements and highlighting areas that need attention. In some cases this work will be done by a support function, freeing the manager to concentrate on decision-making and implementing corrective action.

Project

For a project, the baselines for control will be the business case and the project management plan, i.e. what the project must deliver and how it should be delivered.

Control methods must then be appropriate to the scale, context and complexity of the project.

On many small projects a simple slip chart, comparing actual progress with the baseline on a Gantt chart, will suffice.

On large or complex projects where there is a well-defined scope, a more sophisticated method such as earned value management (EVM) may be needed.

EVM is a project-control process based on a structured approach to planning, cost collection and performance measurement. It is a process that provides benefits for the control of projects. It facilitates the integration of project scope, time and cost objectives in the establishment of a planned schedule and budget baseline and provides the means for comparing the work completed against this baseline.

Conventional scheduling, budgeting and cost management will inform the project manager what budget has been spent and what activities have been completed or are in progress. However, this does not provide a performance measure.

EVM provides this measure of performance and allows future performance to be predicted based on current variances and trends. The purpose of measuring earned value is to provide information in order to determine:

- what has been achieved of the planned work;
- what it has cost to achieve the planned work;
- whether the work achieved is costing more or less than was planned;
- whether the project is ahead or behind the planned schedule.

On projects where time is of the essence and scope is flexible, the Agile approach is becoming increasingly popular. In such projects, the control of time is achieved through timeboxing and the main emphasis is on change control of scope. The MoSCoW technique prioritises requirements within each timebox.

No project will ever run strictly according to plan. A good plan will contain elements of contingency and management reserve that will cushion the effect of issues. Some of these reserves will be in the control of the project manager and others within the control of the project sponsor.

The progress of a project will often be affected by external influences over which the project manager has no control. This is where the project sponsor must provide help and support, and the relationship between the project manager and the project sponsor is vital to effective project control.

Programme

The programme management team do not manage individual projects or detailed change management activities. This is delegated to the project and change management teams.

Defining tolerances is an important part of setting up control systems. These will govern whether something is dealt with at project level or programme level.

Programme level control involves:

- monitoring interdependencies between projects and change management activities;
- tracking key performance indicators to predict where tolerances may be exceeded;
- re-allocating resources and funds to accelerate progress where necessary;
- initiating and closing projects;
- tracking the realisation of benefits;
- conducting post-project, tranche and benefits reviews;
- monitoring the external environment and its effect on the business case.

There will be activity that does not fall within projects or change management. These will include, for example, management of programme-level risks, communication and some procurement. These activities will be monitored against the programme management plan and corrective action taken where necessary.

Although control is the responsibility of the programme manager, it is likely that a support function within the programme will perform the detailed work.

Portfolio

Most of the control in a portfolio is delegated to the projects and programmes. As with any delegated authority, it is important to have clear boundaries and responsibilities.

Portfolio-level control is very similar to programme-level control in that it must:

- monitor interdependencies between projects, programmes and change management activities;
- track key performance indicators to predict where tolerances may be exceeded;
- re-allocate resources and funds to accelerate progress where necessary;
- prioritise, initiate and close projects and programmes;
- balance risk and reward across the portfolio;
- track the realisation of strategic objectives and associated benefits;
- conduct post-project, post-programme and benefits reviews;
- monitor the external environment and its effect on the way the strategic objectives.

Portfolio planning will identify activities for the management of risk, communication, quality, procurement etc. that should be managed at portfolio level. These will form part of the portfolio management plan and are not delegated. Therefore, they will be directly tracked and controlled by the portfolio management team.

Portfolio management must also ensure that control methods are implemented consistently across the portfolio. If this is not done it can be difficult to aggregate data for the whole portfolio and construct an overall picture of progress.

The scale of portfolios will make a support function, such as a portfolio office, essential. This function will perform the data collection, analysis and reporting that enables the portfolio to be controlled. In many cases, the portfolio office may perform the same function for the component programmes and projects.

Further reading

APM Earned Value Specific Interest Group, 2002.
Earned value management: APM guidelines. Princes Risborough: Association for Project Management.

APM Earned Value Specific Interest Group, 2010.
The earned value management compass. Princes Risborough: Association for Project Management.

APM Joint Risk and Earned Value Working Group, 2008.
Interfacing risk and earned value management. Princes Risborough: Association for Project Management.

Maylor, H., 2005.
Project management. London: FT Prentice-Hall.

3.1.3 Information management

Definition

Information management is the collection, storage, dissemination, archiving and destruction of information. It enables teams and stakeholders to use their time, resource and expertise effectively to make decisions and to fulfil their roles.

General

All projects, programmes or portfolios generate data in the course of capturing requirements, planning the work and controlling progress.

P3 management teams need to transform data into information through interpretation, analysis and presentation. They must establish information management processes and responsibilities from the start. These will usually conform to organisational standards, but any adaptation of those standards must be set out in an information management plan.

The information management process starts with data collection and creation, and its conversion to information.

The collection and creation of data takes many forms. In the early stages it will focus on capturing requirements and developing solutions that meet those requirements. It will then move on to the creation of plans showing how the requirements will be met. As the work progresses, performance data will be collected.

Data must be transformed into information that is usable by the P3 management team and stakeholders. This is made easier by adopting standard techniques to analyse the data (such as earned value management to show performance trends) and documents to present the information (such as a business case to show why the investment is worthwhile).

P3 methodologies define a suite of standard documents and many organisations develop electronic templates to ensure consistency. Key documents will be subject to configuration management and the information management plan will define how information is classified and stored.

Storage must be designed with accessibility in mind. Information that cannot be easily found is of no value.

The preparation and dissemination of information will be defined in the communications management plan. This will include ownership, access rights and timing of dissemination.

As information is superseded it must be archived. Archived information needs to provide an audit trail of changes and a source of information in support of lessons learned.

Some archived information may be stored in a knowledge management database that allows easy access in order to help improve the management of future work.

Information that is no longer required will eventually need to be destroyed, subject to statutory requirements and organisational policy. The destruction may be for security or confidentiality reasons, or simply to prevent an accumulation of unnecessary documentation.

Information management processes must comply with related organisational, legal and regulatory standards and policies. Members of the P3 management team will each have a responsibility for aspects of information management.

The P3 assurance process will check that information is being handled in accordance with the information management plan.

Project

Information management can be seen as an overhead that takes time away from managing a project. Many project managers will lack support to help with the administrative burden and, where this is the case, the information management system should be made as simple as possible so that it can be part of the project manager's role.

On larger projects, or where the project is part of a programme, there will probably be a support function that will take care of the information management process. However, the project manager still has responsibility for ensuring that there is an appropriate information management plan in place and that it is implemented.

Where a project is being delivered by one organisation on behalf of another, the project manager must be aware of different policies and conventions that affect the transfer of data and information between the two organisations.

Programme

An information management plan for a programme must address three factors:

- consistency of information management at project level;
- coordination of information management between projects and business-as-usual;
- managing programme-level information.

Consistency across projects is important for both data and information. Data consistency means using a common system for recording and distributing data. This should allow project management teams to have access to relevant information across the programme to better manage their component part. A simple example would be ensuring that all projects in a multinational programme report costs in the same currency, using the same mechanism for calculating exchange rates. Without consistency it is difficult to aggregate information to create an overall picture for the programme.

The programme management team should also ensure that all projects use the same documents, terminology and templates unless there is a compelling reason to do otherwise. This makes communication easier and more efficient.

Some data and reports will only exist at programme level. This will relate to information that is either outside the scope of individual projects, or has been created by aggregating information from multiple sources.

Programmes will often include a support function that can take responsibility for the information management process across projects.

Portfolio

Although united by a set of common strategic goals, the projects and programmes within a portfolio will have different contexts. Wherever possible a portfolio should apply a consistent approach across its component parts but this may be adapted for particular circumstances.

A portfolio support function will handle the information management process and may provide support to all or some of the projects and programmes.

Responsibility for knowledge management and development of maturity is also likely to reside with the portfolio management team. Information management is closely linked with both these areas and information management in the portfolio dimension must take a long-term view to ensure that good practice is embedded in the organisation.

Further reading

International Organization for Standardization, 2009.
[online] Available at: www.apm.org.uk/BoK6FurtherReading.

Laudon, K.C. and Laudon, J.P., 2008.
Management information systems. 11th ed. London: Prentice-Hall.

3.1.4 Organisation

Definition
Organisation is the management structure applicable to the project, programme or portfolio and the organisational environment in which it operates.

General
The organisational structure of individual projects, programmes and portfolios will vary according to the context and specific needs of each situation. In broad terms, the organisation will always have four main levels.

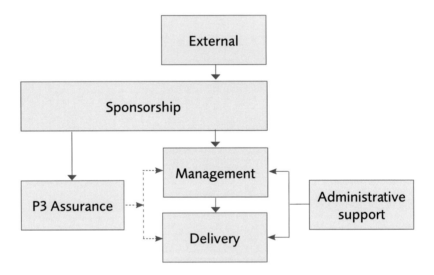

Figure 3.1: Generic organisation structure

The external level represents the host or client organisation for the work. This is the level at which requirements are defined and funding provided. The external organisation delegates responsibility for looking after its interests to the sponsoring level.

Sponsorship is a role that provides a link between the management level and the external environment. The sponsor champions the work and owns the business case.

The management level is where day-to-day responsibility for managing the project, programme or portfolio resides. The management and sponsorship levels collectively comprise the P3 management team.

The delivery level represents those who create the outputs or realise the benefits.

Alongside the four levels are P3 assurance and administrative support.
Assurance reports to the sponsorship level and provides confidence that the management and delivery of the work are being conducted effectively and

appropriately. The administrative support function provides administrative and technical support services to the management and delivery levels.

Temporary project, programme or portfolio organisations may be supported by a permanent governance infrastructure that 'owns' P3 management. This is usually referred to as an enterprise project management office (EPMO).

Most host organisations will be based around a functional structure, i.e. where people work in a particular department. Some project-based organisations, typically in construction or engineering, will have people working exclusively on a particular initiative. The majority of projects and programmes operate in a context that is somewhere between the two; this is known as a matrix organisation.

In a matrix organisation, delivery resources and sometimes management resources report both to their functional manager and to the project or programme. This often creates conflict between the two sources of authority when both impose demands for work to be delivered in the same time frame.

The situation where a functional manager has priority over how resources are used is called a 'weak matrix'. Where a project or programme manager has priority over resources, the structure is known as a 'strong matrix'. Between the two lies the 'balanced matrix'.

From the P3 point of view, the greater the priority that the manager of a project or programme has over the deployment of resources, the more likely it is to succeed.

Project

A project may be stand-alone, part of a programme or within a portfolio; it may be an internal project or delivered by a contractor on behalf of a client. The external level will reflect this context.

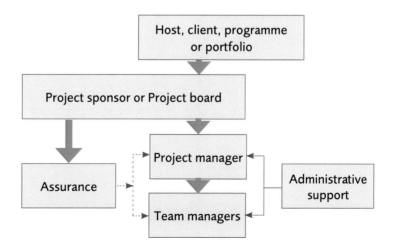

Figure 3.2: Project organisation structure

Sponsorship is normally carried out by an individual who may be supported by other senior managers in a group usually known as a project board or steering group. This is the level that is most affected by the project's environment. For example, where the project is part of a programme, the programme manager may take the role of project sponsor. In the case of a project involving a contractor and client organisation, the project board will include representatives of both.

The project manager looks after day-to-day management and escalates issues to the sponsor or project board.

On large projects there may be team managers appointed to look after work packages. The project manager then delegates responsibility for their day-to-day management to the team managers. Where a project is divided into sub-projects delivered by different contractors, these may, in turn, be managed by the contractors' project managers.

The structure of the project showing contractors, departments, teams and sometimes individuals is often represented by an organisational breakdown structure (OBS). The OBS shows the structure of the project, the communication routes and reporting links.

Through the identification of work packages, an OBS can be combined with a work breakdown structure to produce a responsibility assignment matrix (RAM).

A RAM is used to assign the work packages to the people, organisations or third parties responsible for creating the project's outputs. The RAM can be populated with information regarding whether someone is responsible, or accountable, or should be consulted or informed. This is often known as a RACI chart.

Smaller organisations may lack the capacity to assign individuals exclusively to a project role. In this situation the OBS will reflect the need for individuals to adopt multiple project roles. However, care must be exercised to ensure that the level of risk involved in combining project roles does not become too great.

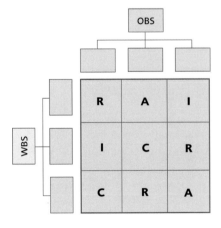

Figure 3.3: RACI chart

In a matrix organisation the project manager may have problems controlling resources that are primarily managed by functional line managers. So there should be negotiated agreements with the functional line managers based on the project schedule. If this approach fails, then the issue is escalated to the sponsor or project board to negotiate on behalf of the project.

The organisational demands of the project may change and should not be seen as constant throughout its life cycle.

Programme

The major addition to the basic organisation structure for programmes is the role of business change manager (BCM). BCMs are responsible for using the outputs of projects to create benefits.

The programme sponsor will invariably be supported by a group of senior managers, known as the sponsoring group, although the sponsor will still be ultimately accountable for the business case.

It is often useful to have, within the sponsoring group, the senior managers from the business units affected by the change; this promotes a closer relationship and understanding between the programme and those affected by it.

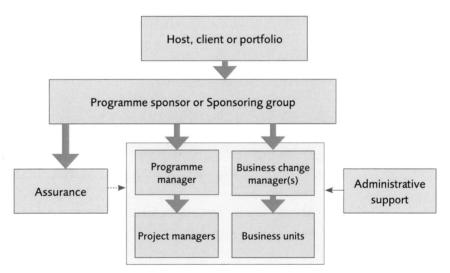

Figure 3.4: Programme organisation structure

A matrix environment at the programme level comprises resources required to deliver benefits, as well as those needed to deliver project outputs. The relationship between programme resources and their departments is an important success factor, so the inclusion of senior business managers on the sponsoring group will help solve any conflicts.

Portfolio

In the portfolio dimension there are typically only three organisational levels, since the external and sponsorship levels are combined.

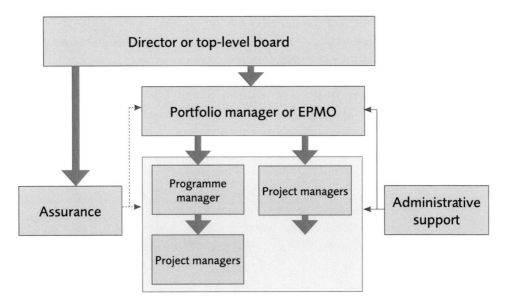

Figure 3.5: Portfolio organisation structure

Ideally, someone on the top-level board of the organisation will represent P3 management. This will effectively make that person the sponsor of the portfolio. If no individual has this responsibility then the complete board should take ownership of the professionalism and discipline of P3 management.

The management of a portfolio may be the responsibility of an individual or of a group sometimes known as an enterprise project management office (EPMO). This is the body that collectively manages the portfolio and is also responsible for the overall development and promotion of P3 management in the host organisation.

As governance of the P3 environment originates at board level, issues surrounding matrix management and the allocation of resources throughout the portfolio can be resolved at the highest level.

Further reading

APM Governance of Project Management Specific Interest Group, 2007.
Co-directing change: a guide to the governance of multi-owned projects.
Princes Risborough: Association for Project Management.

APM Governance of Project Management Specific Interest Group, 2009.
Sponsoring change: a guide to the governance aspects of project sponsorship.
Princes Risborough: Association for Project Management.

APM Governance of Project Management Specific Interest Group, 2011.
Directing change: a guide to governance of project management. 2nd ed.
Princes Risborough: Association for Project Management.

APM ProgM Specific Interest Group, 2007.
APM introduction to programme management. Princes Risborough: Association
for Project Management.

Boddy, D., 2002.
Managing projects: building and leading the team. Harlow: Prentice-Hall.

Lock, D., 2007.
Project management. 9th ed. Aldershot: Gower.

3.1.5 Planning

Definition

Planning determines what is to be delivered, how much it will cost, when it will be delivered, how it will be delivered and who will carry it out.

General

Planning occurs broadly at two levels; policy and delivery.

At the policy level a series of plans set out the principles of how each aspect of the work will be managed. These plans include documents such as the risk management plan, quality management plan and benefits management plan. They are sometimes referred to as strategies (e.g. the benefits management strategy).

The policy-level plans set out procedures and processes for each aspect of management. They list preferred techniques, including templates for documentation and defined responsibilities.

At the delivery level, documents will answer such questions as:

- **Why?** A statement of the reasons the work is required. It includes a definition of the need, problem or opportunity being addressed.
- **What?** Describes the objectives, scope and deliverables of the work, together with their acceptance criteria. It also describes the success criteria for the project and the key performance indicators (KPIs) used to measure success. The 'what' needs to take into account any constraints, assumptions and dependencies.
- **How?** There may be alternative ways of achieving stakeholder requirements. The chosen method should be documented along with reasons for its choice.
- **Who?** The project organisation is defined along with key roles and responsibilities, together with a plan defining the resources that will be required and how they will be acquired.
- **When?** A project schedule that includes key milestones, phasing and detailed timings for the activities required to complete the work.
- **How much?** Including budgets and cash flows for expenditure and, where appropriate, income.
- **Where?** The geographical location(s) where the work will be performed and the impacts on the costs and personnel factors.

All of the delivery information is developed in outline form during the concept phase of a project or programme. This is usually referred to as the project or programme brief.

When senior management give approval to proceed, detailed documentation is prepared in the definition phase. This is then referred to as the project or programme management plan.

On larger projects and all programmes, it is unreasonable to develop detailed schedules for the entire life cycle. The later stages of work will be subject to change, as a result of altered requirements and performance in the earlier stages.

It is common to apply the principle of 'rolling wave planning' where earlier stages and tranches are planned in more detail than the later ones.

It is important to share the management plan with all stakeholders so there is a common understanding of what the requirements are and how they will be delivered.

Although the project or programme manager owns the management plan, it should be developed with the wider team. Some specialist planning expertise may be provided by a support function. This removes ambiguity, sets expectations and develops commitment to the plan.

Once agreed, the management plan provides a baseline which is periodically reviewed and updated with rigorous change control. It forms the basis of gate reviews where the continuing viability of the work is assessed.

By its very nature, delivery planning is speculative. It involves looking into the future and estimating what will happen. Estimates will be based on whatever data is available and expertise in its interpretation and application.

The more data that is available, the more accurate the estimates. Inevitably, in the early phases of a project or programme, there is less data available than in the later phases. This results in an estimating funnel as shown in figure 3.6.

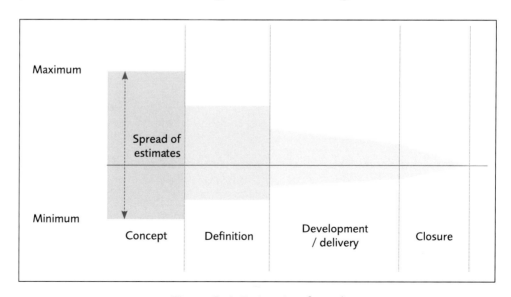

Figure 3.6: Estimating funnel

At the end of each phase, estimates can be refined and the difference between the maximum and minimum reduced.

There are three primary methods of estimating:

- comparative;
- parametric;
- bottom-up.

Comparative, or analogous, estimating uses historical data from similar projects or programmes to extrapolate estimates for new work. Past estimates are scaled according to scope and complexity to produce new estimates.

Comparative estimating is most appropriate when data is available from a few instances of similar work.

Parametric estimating uses defined parameters by which work can be measured (e.g. the area of a building or the number of function points in a computer program) and uses the results to predict values in the current work. Parametric estimating requires an extensive database of past estimates of similar work.

Bottom up, or analytical, estimating uses a detailed specification to estimate time and cost for each component of the work.

Project

When a project is part of a programme or portfolio, or if it is being conducted in a mature P3 management organisation, the team will have access to initial, policy-level planning documents. It is then up to the project management team to tailor these to the specific needs of the project without breaching the principles that provide consistency across the organisation.

Delivery plans will be at their most detailed in the project dimension. Regardless of whether they are stand-alone or part of a programme or portfolio, it is always the projects that deliver the outputs.

Detailed techniques such as product planning for scope, critical path analysis for time scheduling, or Monte Carlo analysis for risk, will be the basis for preparing the project delivery plans.

The output of scope management is a specification that may be presented as a product breakdown structure (PBS) showing the deliverables and a work breakdown structure (WBS) showing the work required to produce them. The planning process will add management activities to the WBS to show the work involved in managing aspects such as risk and communications.

Projects range from the simple to the highly complex. Plans must reflect the nature of the project. Over-complicating the plans of a simple project can be as damaging as over-simplifying the plans of a complex project.

In the early phases of a project, both comparative and parametric estimating methods can be used. As the definition phase develops a product or work breakdown structure, bottom-up estimating can be used.

Single estimates do not allow for human error or limited data. Three-point estimates use optimistic, pessimistic and most likely estimates for packages of work that, in turn, allow a statistical analysis of the overall project estimate.

Programme

The primary focus at programme level is to plan the interdependencies between the component projects and show how project deliverables are transformed into benefits in a timely and productive manner.

The policy-level plans developed by the programme will form the basis of the policy-level plans for each component project. Whilst consistency is desirable, some flexibility is necessary to accommodate the different technical contexts of the projects.

Delivery-level planning must take care not to include too much detail of individual projects and thereby remove autonomy from project management teams. It must focus on key milestones such as deliverables and interdependencies.

Maintaining a consistent planning approach across the programme is an important responsibility of the programme support function, particularly when organisational planning standards have not been prescribed. Consistency is needed to ensure that data from individual projects can be aggregated to provide an overall picture for the programme.

Some benefits realisation will continue once the programme organisation has been disbanded. It is important that benefits realisation plans are formally handed over to the business-as-usual units which will be responsible for continuing benefits realisation.

Programme estimates will comprise two main elements: estimates of the individual projects and estimates of programme and business change activities. The aggregation of estimates from component elements of the programme will represent different phases in the estimating funnel, so great care must be taken in communicating estimates comprising differing degrees of certainty.

Programme planning must set out consistent estimating techniques to allow aggregation where required.

Portfolio

When projects and programmes are delivered through a portfolio, it is important that the portfolio-level planning sets governance standards. The portfolio support function will be responsible for auditing adherence to policies and providing assurance to the portfolio management team that the work is being managed consistently and competently.

High-level planning represents a large part of the portfolio management function. The processes of defining, categorisation, prioritisation and balancing are all largely planning processes. The delivery of outputs and benefits is mostly delegated to the component projects and programmes.

Estimating for the portfolio as a whole would be a largely fruitless process because of the variation in certainty and context of the various projects and programmes. In some cases, it may be possible to aggregate estimates for areas within the portfolio aligned to specific objectives. All such estimates must carry careful explanation of their inherent uncertainty and variability when communicated to stakeholders.

Further reading

British Standards Institution, 2010.
BS 6079-1: 2010 a guide to project management. London, BSI.

Kerzner, H., 2004.
Advanced project management: best practices on implementation. 2nd ed.
Chichester: Wiley.

Lester, A., 2007.
Project management, planning and control. 5th ed. Amsterdam: Elsevier.

Meredith, J.R. and Mantel, S.J., 2010.
Project management: a managerial approach. 7th ed. Hoboken, NJ: Wiley.

Obeng, E., 2002.
Perfect projects. Beaconsfield: Pentacle Works.

Pennypacker, J.S. and Retna, S. eds., 2009.
Project portfolio management - a view from the management trenches. Hoboken,
NJ: Wiley.

Reiss, G. et al., 2006.
The Gower handbook of programme management. London: Gower.

3.1.6 Stakeholder management

Definition
Stakeholder management is the systematic identification, analysis, planning and implementation of actions designed to engage with stakeholders.

General
Stakeholders are individuals or groups with an interest in the project, programme or portfolio because they are involved in the work or affected by the outcomes.

Most projects, programmes and portfolios will have a variety of stakeholders with different, and sometimes competing, interests. These individuals and groups can have significant influence over the eventual success or failure of the work.

Stakeholder management is a set of techniques that harnesses the positive influences and minimises the effect of the negative influences. It comprises four main steps:

- identify stakeholders;
- assess their interest and influence;
- develop communication management plans;
- engage and influence stakeholders.

Identifying stakeholders will be done using research, interviews, brainstorming, checklists, lessons learned and so on. The stakeholders and their areas of interest are usually shown in a table known as a stakeholder map. Typical types of stakeholders will include:

- individuals and groups performing the work;
- individuals and groups affected by the work;
- owners, shareholders and customers;
- statutory and regulatory bodies.

Each stakeholder will then be classified according to potential impact. This is usually shown in a matrix that estimates interest and influence on a simple scale such as low/medium/high. Those with an ability to directly affect the outputs or benefits are sometimes referred to as key stakeholders.

Questions to consider when assessing stakeholders are:

- How will they be affected by the work?
- Will they be openly supportive, negative or ambivalent?
- What are their expectations and how can these be managed?
- Who and/or what influences the stakeholder's view of the project?
- Who would be the best person to engage with the stakeholder?

This analysis is used to develop a communication management plan. Appropriate strategies and actions are then defined to engage with stakeholders in different parts of the matrix.

Communications with stakeholders who have high levels of interest and influence will be managed differently from those with stakeholders of low interest and influence. Similarly, communications with stakeholders who are inherently positive about the work will be different from those with stakeholders who are negative.

P3 managers must identify who should engage with each stakeholder. In many cases the P3 manager will take on the task, but it is also useful to call upon peers, senior managers or others who may be better placed.

As a dynamic document, the communication management plan must link to other plans such as the risk management plan and key milestones within the schedule.

Stakeholder management becomes more complex when stakeholders' views, roles or allegiances, etc. change throughout the life cycle. For that reason, the stakeholder management steps must be repeated throughout the life cycle.

Project

Stakeholder management for a project is the responsibility of the project manager. On larger projects or where the project is part of a programme, there may be assistance from a support function.

Stakeholder management is a vital activity, even on the smallest of projects. Project managers, using simple procedures and investing a modest effort, can make a big difference to the eventual success of the project simply by understanding the stakeholders and what they want.

Programme

Within a programme, stakeholder maps should be created at project and programme level and are the responsibility of the project managers and programme manager respectively.

Stakeholders only appear on maps where they have an interest. So, those with an interest in a project should be on the project-level map. Those with an interest in multiple projects, or the business-as-usual being affected by the projects, should appear on the programme-level map. Where stakeholders have an interest in multiple projects, the programme-level map must differentiate between their interest and influence in each.

This approach ensures that stakeholders appear in only one communication management plan and avoids the danger of mixed messages.

The programme support function will maintain the stakeholder documentation and may include a communications officer. It will also liaise, as appropriate, with either corporate communications or a portfolio support function, where one exists.

Portfolio

The portfolio management team needs to be satisfied that appropriate approaches to stakeholder management are being taken by all projects, programmes and areas of business-as-usual within the portfolio. They must also own and monitor a portfolio-wide stakeholder management plan.

This needs to cover such aspects as:

- the overall stakeholder management policy, including key stakeholder groups and interfaces;
- how the stakeholder management policy will be monitored;
- dealing with perceived weaknesses in stakeholder management at project and programme level;
- gathering and publicising executive support for the portfolio processes and portfolio content.

Stakeholder management is one of the most challenging activities within portfolio management. The overall portfolio of change can be undermined if there are significant areas of an organisation with poor stakeholder commitment.

The portfolio management team is responsible for the quality of local project and programme stakeholder management. Evidence on how well plans are being executed may be reflected in the nature of issues being escalated and risks being reported.

The portfolio support function maintains the stakeholder documentation and may include a communications officer. It will provide guidance to projects and programmes on stakeholder management and will audit stakeholder management throughout the portfolio. It is important that the support function liaises with organisational communications.

Further reading

Armstrong, S. and Beecham, S., 2008.
Studying the interplay between the roles played by stakeholders, requirements and risks in projects. *Project Management Perspectives. The annual publication of the International Project Management Association* 2008,
[online] Available at: www.apm.org.uk/BoK6FurtherReading.

Boddy, D. and Buchannan, D., 1992.
Take the lead: interpersonal skills for project managers. Harlow: FT Prentice-Hall.

Boddy, D., 2002.
Managing projects: building and leading the team. Harlow: Prentice-Hall.

Johnson, G. and Scholes, K., 2004.
Exploring corporate strategy: text and cases. 7th ed. Harlow: FT Prentice-Hall.

Neely, A., Adams, C. and Kennerley, M., 2002.
Performance prism: the scorecard for measuring and managing stakeholder relationships. Harlow: FT Prentice-Hall.

Reiss, G. et al., 2006.
The Gower handbook of programme management. London: Gower.

Young, T.L., 2003.
Handbook of project management. London: Kogan Page.

3.2 **Scope management**

Definition

Scope management is the process whereby outputs, outcomes and benefits are identified, defined and controlled.

General

Scope comprises the totality of the outputs, outcomes and benefits and the work required to produce them. It is the scope of work that is the deciding factor as to whether it will be managed as a project, programme or portfolio.

The way in which scope is managed depends upon two things; the nature of the objectives (outputs, benefits or strategic) and the definability of the objectives.

The scope of a project will typically include outputs, but may be extended to cover benefits. The scope of a programme invariably covers benefits and the resulting change management. The scope of a portfolio is defined by the strategic objectives it is designed to achieve.

Scope management is made up of six main areas that work in unison to identify, define and control the scope:

- requirements management gathers and assesses stakeholder wants and needs. Requirements are 'solution-free', i.e. they describe stakeholders' wants and needs but do not determine exactly how they will be met;
- solutions development takes the stakeholders' requirements and investigates how they may be achieved to provide the best value;
- benefits management takes requirements that have been expressed in terms of benefits and manages them through to their eventual delivery. This runs in parallel with requirements management and solutions development and utilises change management;
- change management deals with the transformation of business- as-usual that is necessary to utilise outputs and realise benefits;
- change control is a mechanism for capturing and assessing potential changes to scope. It ensures that only beneficial changes are made;
- configuration management monitors and documents the development of products. It makes sure that approved changes are recorded and superseded versions archived. The information kept in a configuration management system will help assess the impact of potential changes.

The degree to which detailed requirements and solutions can be predicted at the beginning of the project, programme or portfolio will influence how scope is managed.

Where the objective is well understood and has a tangible output (e.g. in construction and engineering) it is usual to define the scope as accurately as possible at the beginning of the life cycle. This reduces the level of changes that may be required and hence keeps costs from escalating. It is also useful to define what is outside of scope to avoid misunderstandings. Clearly defining what is in and out of scope reduces risk and manages the expectations of all key stakeholders.

Where the objective is less tangible, or subject to significant change, e.g. business change or some IT systems, a more flexible approach to scope is needed. This requires a careful approach to avoid escalating costs.

An important factor in managing the scope of work is to maximise value for money. The discipline of value management brings together an important set of processes and techniques that operate throughout the six areas. It ensures that investment in a project, programme or portfolio is optimised for the potential return it can deliver.

Project

Once a solution has been identified which meets the stakeholder requirements, the scope of the work can be illustrated using a product breakdown structure (PBS) and a work breakdown structure (WBS).

Identifying both products and the work involved in building them is an iterative activity. Where uncertainty about the end products exists, provision must be made for revisiting the PBS and WBS during the project life cycle.

The PBS is a hierarchical structure where the main output of the project is placed at the top level. The next level down shows the components that make up the higher level. This process continues to the level of individual products. Each product will have defined acceptance criteria and quality control methods.

A WBS takes a similar approach but shows the work required to create the products. The lowest level of a WBS shows the activities that would be used to create a network diagram for time scheduling.

In well-defined projects the approved breakdown structures are baselined at the end of the definition phase of the project life cycle. The products in the PBS will become the configuration items for use in configuration management, and any proposed changes of scope will go through a formal change control procedure.

In flexible projects that use an Agile approach, the scope baseline will predominantly comprise functional requirements. The products that fulfil these functions will be developed iteratively throughout the life cycle.

Programme

Programme requirements are typically described in terms of outcomes and benefits. The outputs required to provide the outcomes and benefits, plus the development of solutions for those outputs, are normally delegated to project level.

The relationship between outputs, outcomes and benefits is rarely one-to-one and there will be multiple dependencies between outputs, outcomes and the benefits they enable. As part of managing the scope of the programme these interdependencies must be analysed and documented. Effective value management, solutions development, benefits management, change control and configuration management for the programme as a whole will all depend upon understanding these interdependencies.

Programme scope tends to be fluid. It is unlikely that solutions for all the projects within the programme can be developed at the outset and conditions in the business environment may alter. A programme management team will have to manage evolving scope throughout the life cycle.

Portfolio

The high-level requirements of a portfolio will be defined by the strategic objectives they are designed to satisfy. Its scope is the sum of the projects, programmes and change activity required to deliver those strategic objectives. Scope management of a portfolio is effectively what is done during the define and balance phases of the portfolio life cycle.

When setting up a portfolio it is likely that existing projects and programmes will be included, but these will probably not comprise the full scope of work. Over the life of a portfolio, other ideas for projects and programmes will emerge and compete for inclusion. Each of these will have supporters who believe that their proposal represents the best way to achieve the strategic objectives.

Eligibility criteria need to be established as part of the high-level, portfolio scope definition. These may be expressed in such terms as required levels of return on investment, or acceptable levels of risk, and will be inputs to the requirements management of individual projects and programmes.

Governance arrangements should provide rules for bringing new proposals forward for review, with the portfolio manager helping project and programme sponsors to shape their potential entry into the portfolio.

While solutions development and benefits management are largely delegated to projects and programmes they must be coordinated at the portfolio level to ensure that value is maximised, i.e. the emphasis at portfolio level is on integrated value management.

Further reading

APM Planning Specific Interest Group, 2008.
Introduction to project planning. Princes Risborough: Association for Project Management.

DSDM Consortium, 2008.
The handbook. Ashford: DSDM Consortium.

Harrison, F. and Lock, D., 2004.
Advanced project management: a structured approach. Aldershot: Gower.

Haugan, G.T., 2002.
Effective work breakdown structures. Vienna, VA: Kogan Page.

Kerzner, H., 2009.
Project management: a systems approach to planning, scheduling, and controlling. 10th ed. Hoboken, NJ: Wiley.

Lewis, J.P., 2005.
Project planning, scheduling and control. 4th ed. London: McGraw-Hill.

Project Management Institute, 2001.
Project management institute practice standard for work breakdown structures. Newton Square, PA: Project Management Institute.

Reiss, G. et al., 2006.
The Gower handbook of programme management. London: Gower.

3.2.1 Benefits management

Definition
Benefits management is the identification, definition, planning, tracking and realisation of business benefits.

General
Delivering benefits is the primary reason why organisations undertake change. A benefit is a positive and measurable impact of change. However, in some cases there may be unavoidable negative impacts of change that are acceptable in the context of greater benefits. These are called disbenefits.

Benefits can be tangible (e.g. money saved, jobs created) or intangible (e.g. corporate reputation, capacity for change). They may, or may not, also be quantifiable in cash terms (e.g. reduced costs or greater customer satisfaction).

The forecast benefits of a programme or project are the basis of its business case. The sponsor owns the business case and is ultimately accountable for the realisation of the benefits.

In a cost/benefit analysis the costs are definitely tangible and quantifiable. The tangible and quantifiable benefits will ideally outweigh the costs. It is dangerous to rely too much on intangible and unquantifiable benefits to justify expenditure.

Benefits-driven change requires proactive management throughout the entire life cycle. An organisation identifies the benefits it needs and initiates changes that are forecast to deliver benefits. During the change, the organisation needs to monitor performance indicators that can reliably predict benefits delivery.

Day-to-day responsibility for the implementation of change and realisation of benefits lies with one or more business change managers. The relationship between the project or programme manager and the business change manager is crucial. The delivery of outputs and the management of change must be closely coordinated.

Benefits management is an iterative process with five main steps as illustrated in figure 3.7.

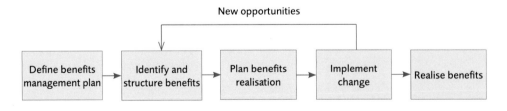

Figure 3.7: Benefits management process

Define benefits management plan: This explains how benefits will be managed. It sets out policies for aspects such as measurement, roles and responsibilities, priorities and key performance indicators (KPIs).

Identify and structure benefits: Requirements are captured from sources such as the project mandate and stakeholders. Benefits depend on the delivery of outputs and the achievement of outcomes. The interrelationships between these need to be understood through benefits modelling and mapping. Each benefit (and disbenefit) should be documented in terms of priority, interdependencies, value, timescales and ownership.

Plan benefits realisation: This step involves capturing baseline measurements and agreeing targets. Baseline measurements identify the current performance of an operation so that improvements can be measured. The benefits plan illustrates the timeline and milestones for realising benefits, including any dependencies on project outputs or interactions between benefits.

Implement change: Benefits happen when something changes. This usually involves permanently changing attitudes and behaviours as well as physical changes. While implementing change, new opportunities for additional benefits should always be sought.

Realise benefits: Changes to the way people work need to be embedded to ensure that benefits continue to be realised. A business change manager needs to track realisation and ensure that the change is permanent. The bulk of the benefits may only be realised after a project or programme is completed. Long-term actions and monitoring for continued realisation should be documented as part of the handover to business-as-usual.

Project

In most cases the project ends with the delivery of an output. However, some projects will continue through the extended project life cycle to deliver measurable benefits. A project needs to be clear from the outset whether it is delivering outputs or benefits. This will govern how the project is constituted and managed.

Where a project is only responsible for delivering outputs, it must interface with whoever is responsible for delivering the benefits. This may be a programme, portfolio or business-as-usual organisation.

Programme

The benefits associated with strategic organisational change are delivered through programmes of multiple-aligned projects and change management activity. Such programmes can contain complex interactions between the outputs of individual projects, outcomes and benefits.

The attribution of programme benefits to individual projects and double counting of benefits across a programme can be difficult issues, particularly where investment approvals are impacted. These should be approached in a pragmatic way and resolved through effective mapping and stakeholder consultation. Where appropriate, the benefit should be attributed to a specific project based on the principle of greatest contribution.

It is important to implement a consistent approach to benefits management across a programme, particularly for consistency of measurement. Without a consistent approach, it is difficult to aggregate benefits across multiple projects and assess their collective impact on business performance across the organisation.

Portfolio

A portfolio will deliver a collection of strategically-aligned benefits. It will do this through its component projects and programmes. Strategy mapping helps ensure that investment decisions, and the scope of each project and programme, are driven by the contribution of benefits to achieving the operational, organisational or business strategy.

A portfolio must have a consistent set of guidelines for benefits management practices for all programmes and projects, including tracking, forecasting and reporting. This enables benefits to be compared and aggregated across the portfolio. It also helps to minimise double counting and facilitates an even-handed investment appraisal. This is essential for the categorise, prioritise and balance phases of the portfolio life cycle.

A well-defined and flexible, portfolio-wide, policy for benefits management will greatly reduce the work needed to develop governance policies at project and programme level.

At a portfolio level, it is possible to make use of data on the performance of benefits management (e.g. optimism bias, which is the tendency to overestimate benefits and underestimate costs). This can be used to improve benefits management practices by sharing and applying lessons learned.

Further reading

APM Benefits Management Specific Interest Group, 2009.
Benefits management: a strategic skill for all seasons.
[online] Available at: www.apm.org.uk/BoK6FurtherReading.

APM Benefits Management Specific Interest Group, 2010.
Benefits realisation: what are your chances of success?
[online] Available at: www.apm.org.uk/BoK6FurtherReading.

APM Benefits Management Specific Interest Group, 2010.
From physical change to benefits in the built environment: the rationale for success.
[online]. Available at: www.apm.org.uk/BoK6FurtherReading.

Bradley, G., 2010.
Benefit realisation management. 2nd ed. Farnham: Gower.

Bradley, G., 2010.
Fundamentals of benefit realization. Norwich: The Stationery Office.

Reiss, G. et al., 2006.
The Gower handbook of programme management. London: Gower.

3.2.2 Change control

Definition

Change control is the process through which all requests to change the baseline scope of a project, programme or portfolio are captured, evaluated and then approved, rejected or deferred.

General

In traditional development models where scope is well defined early in the life cycle, it is essential for success that changes to baselined scope are controlled. A rigorous change control process must be established and maintained on all projects, programmes and portfolios.

The process must allow all stakeholders to submit their suggestions for changes to scope and typically comprises five steps:

Request: The stakeholder who requests a change must provide relevant information on the nature of the change. The request is entered into a change register which records all requests and their status (e.g. pending, approved, rejected or deferred).

Review: The change request is reviewed to determine its high-level impact on outputs and benefits. If necessary, further clarification may be sought before deciding if it is worthwhile performing a detailed assessment. The proposed change may be rejected without further evaluation, in which case the reasons for rejection will be recorded and the stakeholder informed

Assessment: All options relating to the change are captured and evaluated. The detailed impact on plans and schedules is estimated and a recommendation to approve, reject, defer, or request more information is made. Thresholds are set to determine whether the decision can be made by the P3 manager, sponsor or other members of the management team.

Decision: The decision is communicated to the team and stakeholders as outlined in the communication management plan and the configuration management plan.

Implementation: Relevant plans and schedules are updated if a change is approved and before the changes are made to existing products, or specifications for future products.

If an unauthorised or emergency change is identified, it should be retrospectively put through the change control process.

Change control is intrinsically linked to configuration management. Any changes need to be fed back into the configuration management system. In certain circumstances, it may be appropriate to have a change freeze where no further changes to scope will be considered. Where this has been agreed by the sponsor, it should be included as a key decision point in the configuration management plan.

Project

Most change control happens at project level as this is where tangible products are delivered.

If the project has an agreed change budget, it may be in the control of the project manager who will make decisions about accepting or refusing change requests. If changes are major or cumulatively exceed the budget, then they may have to be escalated to the project sponsor for funding from the management reserve.

Change requests often take on a contractual significance where a project is being delivered by a contractor for a client. Contract terms will dictate a change control process that governs how the contractor will be paid for changes to the specification on which the original price was agreed.

In some industries, schedules of rates form the basis of pricing changes in advance of implementation. This eliminates the need to negotiate a price between contractor and client. Uncontrolled change in a contractual environment often leads to claims that may have to be settled in court.

Agile projects make change control an integral part of the development process. Each development iteration starts with a planning meeting that clarifies and prioritises the function addressed in the iteration. Some of these features may be changes to existing features but are considered alongside all the others.

Programme

Programmes are primarily concerned with changes that relate to benefits, either directly or indirectly through a change to a project's output. The change control process at programme level will initially assess the impact of a change request on benefits and then assess the impact on the component projects. Significant change to a project may require a redistribution of resources or funds and may have a knock-on effect on other projects.

The programme management team may also be involved in project change requests that have an effect on other projects. The interrelationships between projects must be well mapped so that the impact of change requests that affect multiple projects can be assessed properly.

Portfolio

Major changes are escalated to the portfolio management team from projects and programmes. They will need to consider how any portfolio-level management reserve will be used to fund major changes.

The scale of a portfolio means that it is subject to changes in organisational strategy. This, in turn, might result from changes to the portfolio's environment. Any changes at this level will need to be communicated down to the individual projects and programmes, together with an analysis to determine their impact.

Further reading

APM Earned Value Specific Interest Group, 2002.
Earned value management: APM guidelines. Princes Risborough: Association for Project Management.

Field, M. and Keller, L., 1998.
Project management. Andover: Cengage Learning EMEA.

Lock, D., 2007.
Project management. 9th ed. Aldershot: Gower.

3.2.3 Configuration management

Definition
Configuration management encompasses the administrative activities concerned with the creation, maintenance, controlled change and quality control of the scope of work.

General
A configuration is the set of functional and physical characteristics of a final deliverable defined in the specification and achieved in the execution of plans. Configuration management can be regarded as asset control and is essential whether or not multiple versions of a deliverable will be created. At its simplest, configuration management is version control.

Configuration management is an invaluable tool for providing control of the deliverables and avoiding mistakes and misunderstandings. It is an integral part of quality management.

The process ensures that the deliverable meets the specified performance criteria. It also ensures that adequate process is in place to provide continuing maintenance for the duration of the product life cycle.

There are five activities within a configuration management process:

- configuration management planning: A configuration management plan should describe any specific procedures and the extent of their application during the life cycle. The plan should also identify roles and responsibilities for carrying out configuration management. Configuration management must be planned in order to be effective, predictable and repeatable;
- configuration identification: This involves breaking down the work into component deliverables (configuration items), creating a unique numbering or referencing system and establishing configuration baselines;
- configuration control: This ensures that all changes to configuration items are documented. An important aspect is the ability to identify the interrelationships between configuration items. This is essential information for the 'review' and 'assessment' steps in the change control process;
- configuration status accounting: This tracks the current status of a configuration, providing traceability of configuration items throughout their development and operation;

- configuration verification and audit: This is used to determine whether a deliverable conforms to its requirements and configuration information. Typically, an audit is undertaken at the end of a phase, stage or tranche.

A configuration audit will take one of three forms:

- a physical audit looks at the relevant elements of a configuration item and will confirm that the item meets its specification. It will check the results of quality control and confirm that all the necessary test documentation has been completed;
- a functional audit of a configuration item will check that it performs the function for which it was designed;
- a system audit checks that the configuration management system is working and able to support the process and perform the necessary functions.

Configuration management is very closely aligned with change control. Together, these two processes ensure that deliverables meet the required specification, any changes are beneficial changes and there is a complete audit trail for the development of each deliverable.

While the configuration is primarily concerned with the products of a project or programme, it should also be applied to key management documents. For example, a document such as a business case should be subject to version control and audit to ensure that it is fit for purpose and all changes are recorded.

As work is completed, responsibility for maintaining deliverables passes to business-as-usual. The project or programme management team is responsible for ensuring that configuration management information is suitable for transfer to those who will be maintaining the products long after the project or programme has been closed.

Project

Most configuration management is performed at project level because that is where the most tangible deliverables are produced. The configuration management plan will probably form part of the quality management plan but may be separate in large or complex projects.

The product breakdown structure (PBS), plus detailed descriptions of each product, becomes the configuration. Once this is baselined it is subject to formal change control and configuration management.

In agile projects the initial configuration will be very flexible and updated frequently. The lack of a full and detailed configuration at the start makes configuration management of vital importance in this highly dynamic environment.

Programme

A key objective of configuration management is to ensure that all component products fit together and function properly in combination. Therefore, each project and activity within the programme must adopt a consistent approach to managing configurations. This makes it much simpler to assess whether an upgrade or change to the products of one project will have any knock-on effect for the products of another project, or on the programme's eventual benefits.

To ensure a consistent approach, it is normal to publish a programme-level configuration management plan and ensure its effective implementation by all project and business change managers.

Accurate recording of the test status is especially important when products from different projects are combined. Particularly in safety critical, secure or related environments, a key role of the programme is to ensure that there are no gaps in the chain of quality control, testing and record keeping throughout all the products, intermediate assemblies and testing regimes that might compromise the final programme-level deliverables.

Portfolio

It is beneficial for all projects and programmes within a portfolio to operate consistent configuration management systems. Where a portfolio is made up of projects and programmes of similar technical content, a portfolio view of the collective configurations can highlight reusable components.

The portfolio itself is unlikely to produce any configuration items other than key management documents.

Further reading

British Standards Institution, 2010.
British Standards Institution, 2010. BS 6079-1: 2010 a guide to project management.
London, BSI.

Brooks, F.P., 1995.
The mythical man month and other essays on software engineering. 2nd ed. White
Plains, NY: Addison-Wesley.

Field, M. and Keller, L., 1997.
Project management. Andover: Cengage Learning EMEA.

Reiss, G. et al., 2006.
The Gower handbook of programme management. London: Gower.

3.2.4 Change management

Definition

Change management is a structured approach to moving an organisation from the current state to the desired future state.

General

The conversion of outputs into outcomes and benefits invariably requires some form of organisational change. Resistance to change is a natural phenomenon, so managing change in a structured and controlled manner is essential if the benefits in a business case are to be realised.

Organisations respond to change in many different ways. One way of understanding how an organisation may react to change is through metaphors. Morgan identified eight organisational metaphors that include regarding an organisation as a machine, an organism or a political system.

There are many change management models, such as those of Kotter, Carnall and Lewin. Each model has a different approach and applies different metaphors. Carnall's model, for example, is applicable to organisations that operate like a political system but not those that operate like a machine, whereas Lewin's model is the reverse.

A typical, generic, change management process might include the following steps, each of which resonates with the P3 environment and processes.

Figure 3.8: Change management process

In P3 management the assess step constitutes what is needed to convert outputs into outcomes and benefits.

The prepare step involves creating a vision and gaining support. This would form part of the concept phase of a project or programme. This is when stakeholder management is used to gain support for the outline business case, with particular emphasis on changes required to business-as-usual. In the definition phase of a project or programme, this would also include establishing governance and roles to support change, such as the appointment of business change managers.

The plan step is a familiar process to both P3 managers and change managers. The various P3 plans and schedules must take change into account, particularly in the communication management plan and the risk management plan.

The implement step is the heart of the process. It includes communicating the benefits of the change, removing obstacles and coordinating the activities that transform business-as-usual from the status quo to the new way of working. Much depends on the organisation's readiness for change. This is represented by three key factors:

- dissatisfaction with the current situation (A);
- desirability of the proposed change (B);
- practicality of the proposed change (D).

These factors are often included in the formula:

$$C = (ABD) > X$$

This demonstrates the fact that, for change (C) to be successful, the combination of A, B and D must be greater than the cost of the change (X).

For changes to deliver the benefits required by the business case, they have to be stable and become the normal way of working. The sustain step will continue beyond the P3 life cycle to ensure that value is continually realised from the investment in the project, programme or portfolio.

Project

Projects often conclude with the delivery of an output that is handed over to the client or user organisation. The latter then takes responsibility for any change management required to ensure that benefits accrue from the output.

This does not necessarily mean that the project has no responsibility for change management. The project management team can support the assessment, preparation and planning steps of the change management process and coordinate with the change management team to facilitate implementation.

Where the output of a project and resulting benefit are independent of any other outputs and benefits, then responsibility for benefits management and the change management component may be included in an extended project life cycle.

Programme

Programmes invariably involve significant change. This needs to be coordinated across multiple projects and business-as-usual units. The programme organisation is set up to place equal emphasis on the delivery of outputs and the management of change that realises the benefits.

At the outset of a programme it is not easy to predict all the necessary change. The concept of a programme vision and blueprint forms an essential part of the 'assess' and 'prepare' steps of the change management process.

Early communication and promotion of the vision will help to develop an understanding of the desirability and practicality of the change from an early stage.

A common obstacle to change is the volume of change imposed on individuals, teams or business units. The programme management team should structure the tranches of the programme and coordinate the project schedules to ensure that change comes in manageable pieces.

Benefits reviews within a programme must focus on sustainability of the changes implemented to ensure that long-term goals in the business case are achieved.

Portfolio

The portfolio management team's role in change management is one of coordination, validation and governance.

Coordination involves overseeing the change management plans of all projects and programmes in the portfolio to ensure that they work together effectively. For example, if multiple projects and programmes are imposing change on a single business unit this can have a negative effect, either because the unit cannot accommodate that level of change or because the multiple changes counteract each other.

Validation is ensuring that all the change implemented is consistent with the strategic objectives of the portfolio.

Governance involves setting policies for how change will be managed. If different projects, programmes or business units set about change in different ways for no justifiable reason, it can create discord across the organisation as a whole.

Further reading

Alvesson, M., 2002.
Understanding organizational culture. London: Sage. Ch.8.

Balogun, J., Hope-Hailey, V., Johnson, G. and Scholes, K., 2008.
Exploring strategic change (exploring corporate strategy). London: FT Prentice-Hall.

3.2.5 Requirements management

Definition
Requirements management is the process of capturing, assessing and justifying stakeholders' wants and needs.

General
A clear and agreed expression of requirements and their acceptance criteria is essential for the success of any project, programme or portfolio. Requirements may be expressed as physical deliverables or business benefits, as aspirations or solutions, and as functional or technical needs.

The first step in the process is to gather all types of requirements. Most requirements will be generated by internal and external stakeholders, such as clients and users, but there will be a background of legal or regulatory requirements that must also be included.

The various requirements are assessed to ensure they are practical, achievable, and define what is needed rather than how they will be achieved. A well specified requirement is:

- uniquely identifiable: it addresses only one core requirement;
- current: it is up to date and relevant to the business need;
- consistent: it does not contradict any other requirement;
- understandable: concisely stated and not open to different interpretations;
- verifiable: compliance can be verified through inspection, demonstration, test or analysis;
- traceable: the requirement can be traced from the originating need, through the plan, to what is delivered;
- prioritised: its relative importance is understood.

A simple process for requirements management has four steps:

- gather requirements from stakeholders;
- analyse the requirements to look for overlaps, gaps and conflicts;
- justify the requirements to distinguish wants from needs;
- baseline the needs before commencing the solutions development process.

These steps will be undertaken in different ways, depending on sector practice and the individual development methodologies used. For example, the approach for software development using Agile methods would be different from that using a waterfall approach; managing requirements for business transformation will be different from construction.

Value management is an established, structured approach to both requirements management and solutions development. This is a consultative approach that focuses on the value that can be generated by stakeholder requirements.

Value is a subjective term and means different things to different people. In the P3 environment it is a means of maximising value for money and is represented by the ratio where value is proportional to the satisfaction of requirements divided by the use of resources.

The goal of value management is not to maximise the satisfaction of requirements, nor to minimise the use of resources, but to establish the balance that maximises the ratio.

The first four steps of a value management process that relate to requirements management are shown in figure 3.9.

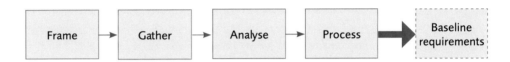

Figure 3.9: Value management process

Framing the work involves establishing the high-level principles within which requirements will be managed. It will establish how functions such as stakeholder management, risk management and resource management will be integrated with requirements management to maximise value.

This step also involves an early assessment of the high-level requirements by developing a value profile that estimates the relative contribution to the value of each requirement.

The gathering of requirements can be done in any number of ways. It ranges from personal interviews, surveys and workshops, to focus groups, modelling and simulation.

Some methodologies, including Agile approaches, are designed to enable the continuous gathering and refinement of requirements on the assumption that the stakeholders may not be sure of their needs.

One of the advantages of a formal method, such as value management, is that it provides lessons learned that can be used to review how similar requirements may have been managed previously.

Analysing requirements combines information from functions such as schedule management and investment appraisal with specific value-based techniques such as function analysis and function cost analysis. The result is a thorough understanding of requirements and the value they contribute to the overall objective.

The 'process' step is primarily about providing feedback to stakeholders, building consensus, and generating ideas. The results of the analysis are communicated through individual consultation or group workshops. This leads to a debate about functionality and alternative ideas. The result is a baselined set of options for functional requirements. These can then be used to examine the value of alternative solutions during solutions development.

Project

High-level requirements are defined during the concept phase of the project life cycle. These need to be detailed enough to complete a project brief. This, in turn, is used to make an investment decision (i.e. whether or not to proceed to the definition phase).

The level of detail captured during the concept phase, therefore, needs to be sufficient to justify proceeding to the definition phase.

For projects that are part of a programme, these high-level requirements will be derived from the programme requirements. They will relate to an output and, if the programme requirements are sufficiently well described, the process may be correspondingly brief, as it simply needs to add the final details.

For stand-alone projects the first consideration is whether the requirements are expressed as outputs, outcomes or benefits. This will govern whether the project includes benefits realisation as part of an extended project life cycle.

Some methodologies, including Agile approaches, are designed to enable the continuous gathering and refinement of requirements on the assumption that the stakeholders may not be sure of their needs at the outset.

In an Agile project the requirements management process must be efficient and dynamic. It must use rigorous prioritisation mechanisms, such as MoSCoW, to ensure that only valuable and justifiable requirements are included in each phase of work.

Programme

Programme requirements will be expressed as benefits. Deciding outputs that will be required to deliver the benefits is an aspect of solutions development, but as each output is defined, requirements management will be used to gather and analyse detailed requirements for the output.

The programme management team is responsible for requirements management as it applies to the programme's benefits. In this respect, requirements management runs concurrently with the early stages of benefits management. The team must then decide how much responsibility for requirements management will be delegated to the project teams.

Where value management is implemented, the programme management team must balance value across the projects. For example, the distribution of resources may result in greater overall value being generated across the programme, even though this appears to reduce value from the perspective of a particular project.

A common dividing line between the programme and projects is that the programme will express the functional requirements needed from an output in order to realise the required benefits. It is then for the project team to manage the technical requirements that will deliver the required functionality.

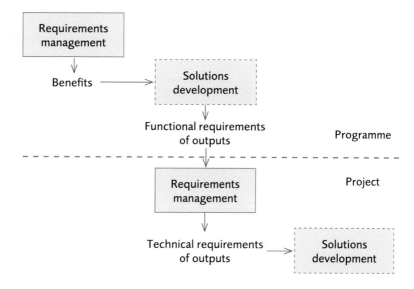

Figure 3.10: Relationship between project and programme requirements management

During the concept phase of a programme the main focus will be on establishing the key benefits of the programme, but it will also be necessary to identify possible projects, with initial estimates of cost, in order to prepare a draft business case.

When a programme is given the go-ahead to continue to the definition phase, the requirements management process will refine the understanding of the benefits. This phase of the programme life cycle will also perform requirements management for the projects in the first tranche of the programme in order to develop a more detailed business case.

Portfolio

The top-level requirements of a portfolio will be expressed in terms of the organisation's strategic objectives. These will be a mixture of stand-alone and interrelated requirements. The requirements management process at portfolio level assesses the strategic objectives and clarifies them with the executive board.

The assessment of requirements will be central to the definition phase of the portfolio life cycle, as interrelated objectives may be collected into a programme and stand-alone objectives delivered through projects. This will contribute to the definition and categorisation phases of the portfolio life cycle.

Most requirements management activity will be delegated to the project and programme management teams, but the portfolio management team must perform three key functions:

1. The team act as the interface between the projects and programmes, on the one hand, and the executive board which owns the strategy, on the other. On behalf of the executive board, the portfolio management team must ensure that its requirements are accurately translated into projects and programmes. On behalf of the project and programme management teams, it must ensure that the strategic requirements are adequately defined so that the projects and programmes have sufficient information to deliver the right outputs and benefits.
2. The team must coordinate projects and programmes to ensure that the many, localised, requirements management processes work in harmony. This may involve taking central responsibility for dealing with key stakeholders; it will involve vetting detailed project and programme requirements to monitor gaps, overlaps and conflicts.
3. Applying value management will enable the prioritising and balancing processes in the portfolio life cycle to make decisions based on the value generated by the different projects and programmes.

Further reading

BCS, The Chartered Institute for IT, 2010.
Business analysis. 2nd ed. Swindon: BISL.

BCS Requirements Engineering Specialist Group, 2010. Requirements quarterly: RQ54 [online]. Available at www.apm.org.uk/BoK6FurtherReading.

BCS Requirements Engineering Specialist Group, 2010. Requirements quarterly: RQ55 [online]. Available at www.apm.org.uk/BoK6FurtherReading.

BCS Requirements Engineering Specialist Group, 2011. Requirements quarterly: RQ56 [online]. Available at www.apm.org.uk/BoK6FurtherReading.

DSDM Consortium, 2008.
The handbook. Ashford: DSDM Consortium.

Forsberg, K., Mooz, H. and Cotterman, H., 2000.
Visualising project management: a model for business and technical success. 2nd ed. Chichester: Wiley.

Pidd, M., 2004.
Systems modelling: theory and practice. Chichester: Wiley.

Robertson, S. and Robertson, J., 2006.
Mastering the requirements process. Harlow: Addison-Wesley.

Stevens, R., Brook, P., Jackson, K. and Arnold, S., 1998.
Systems engineering: coping with complexity. Harlow: Addison-Wesley.

3.2.6 Solutions development

Definition

Solutions development is the process of determining the best way of satisfying requirements.

General

A simple requirements management process produces a clear set of baselined stakeholder requirements. A more sophisticated value management approach produces a baseline that includes ideas for alternative functionality that would be acceptable to stakeholders. Either way the baseline requirements do not explain how to meet the requirements.

Solutions development explores the options for how to meet requirements and then implements the best solution. In broad terms, solutions development comprises the three steps shown in figure 3.11.

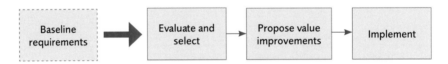

Figure 3.11: Solutions development process

Evaluation and selection looks at all the ideas and assesses how well they will perform against stated criteria such as reduced capital cost, speed of delivery or level of risk. Techniques such as value for money ratios, value trees and value engineering can be used to help select the best value options.

Some options may call for innovation. Strategies to exploit innovation include:

- prototyping – exploring the innovation offline, for example by 'technology demonstrator' projects or 'rapid applications development';
- the use of modelling, simulation and synthetic environments;
- phased implementation of new technology.

The emerging solution is subject to periodic reviews and ultimately results in the issue of a specification that can be used to build a detailed business case. In some cases, the detailed specification will only cover the early stages of development, with later stages being refined as the work proceeds. The development of value-improving proposals can occur at any stage of delivering a project or programme. A key idea from systems engineering is the progressive testing of the emerging products against the expectations laid down in the specification and requirements.

'Verification' is the term used to ensure that the solution is being built right; 'validation' is the term used to ensure that the right product is being built. Validation is against requirements; verification is against specifications.

Project

A project is concerned with delivering a tangible output. In a traditional project this will be described in a specification that is part of the project management plan. It is approved at the end of the definition phase and its components articulated in a product breakdown structure (PBS).

Where there needs to be flexibility in the specification and an opportunity to refine the solution regularly, an Agile approach is more appropriate. In Agile projects a solution may be described mainly in terms of its functionality, with technical specifications being developed during short delivery stages known as sprints. Each sprint is typically two to six weeks long.

Programme

The specified solution for a programme is usually referred to as the 'blueprint'. This describes all aspects of the organisation as it will appear and operate once the programme is complete. This could include organisational structures, business processes, physical infrastructure and information requirements.

Each project within the programme is aimed at delivering an aspect of the blueprint. In most cases the degree of detail in the blueprint will leave ample space for project teams to consider alternative solutions at the project level.

The programme management team coordinate project solutions and identify solution elements. These are elements such as common components and technology platforms that are transferable between projects. The compatibility of solutions proposed by different projects also needs to be checked at programme level.

Portfolio

Developing a solution is very much a project or programme responsibility. The portfolio management team may wish to set guidelines about innovation and risk that constrain the types of solution that can be considered. Where value management is applied, this may involve setting criteria for the evaluation and selection of functionality across the entire portfolio, or for categories of projects and programmes within the portfolio.

Where innovation is the norm, the portfolio must seek to maximise the advantage of successful innovation by seeking to apply it in all relevant parts of the portfolio.

Further reading

Adair, J., 2010.
Decision making and problem solving strategies. London: Kogan Page.

Larman, C., 2004.
Agile and iterative development: a manager's guide. London: Addison-Wesley.

Shore, J., 2007.
The art of agile development. Farnham: O'Reilly.

3.3 **Schedule management**

Definition
Schedule management is the process of developing, maintaining and communicating schedules for time and resource.

General
A schedule is the timetable for a project, programme or portfolio. It shows how the work will progress over a period of time and takes into account factors such as limited resources and estimating uncertainty.

The scheduling process starts with the work that is needed to deliver stakeholder requirements. This includes the technical work that creates outputs, the change management work that delivers benefits, and the management activity that handles aspects such as risk management and stakeholder management.

Some types of work can be defined much more easily than other types. The work involved in building a house is clear from the start. The work involved in maintaining a generator is not clear until inspections are complete. Engineering work tends to have complete specifications from the start, whereas change management and some IT work follow a more iterative approach to defining what needs to be done.

Approaches to calculating schedules have to be equally flexible. In some cases, rigorous techniques can be used to model the work and calculate detailed timings. In other cases, broad estimates have to be made initially, with constant refinement as more information becomes available.

A detailed model can be used to perform 'what-if' calculations to test the result of potential events (e.g. 'What if resource x is not available in February?', or 'What if there is adverse weather in March?').

The detailed and high-level scheduling approaches are both combined in 'rolling wave' scheduling. Short-term work is typically the best defined and can be subject to the most rigorous scheduling. Longer-term work is more vague and subject to change. The window of detail moves along the schedule like a rolling wave.

Schedules are presented in many different ways in order to suit the circumstances. The choice of presentation will depend upon:

- the level of detail required;
- whether time and/or resource is being shown;
- the context of the work (e.g. construction, IT, engineering or business change);
- the dimension being scheduled (project, programme or portfolio);
- the target audience.

The most common form of graphical schedule is the Gantt chart. In its simplest form this uses bars on a horizontal timescale to show the start, duration and finish of packages of work. Variants of the Gantt chart can convey all manner of information to suit the circumstances.

A communication management plan is used to explain who is to receive scheduling information and when. The choice of presentation is tailored to the recipients.

Schedules are contained within the P3 management plan. The schedules that form part of the approval of the work become the baseline against which progress is tracked.

Schedules are fundamental to the control of the project, programme or portfolio. Care must be taken in selecting modelling and calculation techniques, forms of presentation and software tools. Scheduling policies will be set out in the P3 management plan so that scheduling is consistent and widely understood.

On conclusion of the work, schedules that show what was planned and what actually happened are an important resource in determining lessons learned.

Project

Outputs are produced at project level and this is where the most detailed scheduling can take place. The approach to scheduling will depend upon the nature of the project in relation to the triple constraints of time, cost and scope.

Some projects may have to be delivered by a specific date, others within a limited budget, or using limited resources. Some projects may have a very well-defined scope of work and others may intend to develop the scope iteratively throughout the life cycle (often known as Agile project management).

Where there is a well-defined scope of work it will often be presented as a work breakdown structure (WBS) showing how major packages of work are progressively broken down into individual activities.

Schedule management runs in parallel with other processes such as scope management, risk management and quality management. In the early parts of the project life cycle the amount of detailed information available is limited. A schedule may be restricted to indicating target dates for major milestones. As these cannot be calculated from a detailed description of work, the milestone dates may initially be estimated using comparative or parametric forms of estimating.

Once scope management has identified the work required, a detailed model can be built showing how the work will be performed. Various methods can be used on the model to calculate the start and finish dates of all the component activities. Some of these methods only consider the estimated time required to perform each piece of work, while others will allow resources and productivity rates to be included.

Traditionally, the schedule concentrates on the technical activity of delivering the project's output. It is becoming increasingly common to include management activity in the schedule, such as communications activity, quality control activity or risk response activity. In some cases these are combined into a complete schedule and sometimes there are separate schedules, although there must be a mechanism for monitoring dependencies between schedules.

Programme

A programme schedule should not be simply an accumulation of detail from the component project schedules. Within a programme there will be:

- projects that are under way and have their own detailed schedules;
- projects that are in the early stages of definition;
- projects that are yet to be initiated;
- programme management activity;
- change management activity in relation to outputs that have been delivered;
- change management activity in relation to outputs being developed.

This variety of types and detail of activity must be collected into an effective and manageable programme schedule.

First of all, the programme must define a consistent approach to scheduling that will be used across the programme. This includes consistent techniques for estimating and calculating schedules, consistent software tools and a consistent approach to summarising information for inclusion in the programme schedule.

Ideally, the programme schedule will include milestones from the project schedules and the change management activity. In particular it must include interdependencies between different projects and other work.

The programme schedule not only provides estimates of the timing and resource usage of the programme, it must also enable decisions to be made about the acceleration and deceleration of work within the programme. Individual projects will be focused on their designated targets. Sometimes, a programme management team will need to divert resources from one project to another in the overall interests of the programme.

Portfolio

A portfolio schedule must encompass a very wide range of work with greatly varying degrees of detail and accuracy. Portfolio schedules must always be communicated in a way that enables stakeholders to understand what information is derived from detailed schedules and what is more speculative.

An important function of the portfolio management team is a version of capacity planning. Portfolio management must ensure that the necessary resources can be procured to deliver the portfolio. It must also avoid bottlenecks and conflicting demands on limited resources. This means estimating the number of resources required and the timing of their utilisation.

The balancing phase of the portfolio life cycle must constantly review changing resource demands and prioritise the allocation of limited resources. Doing this effectively will depend upon the schedule information aggregated from the component projects and programmes.

Ideally, the portfolio support function will provide scheduling expertise to all the component projects and programmes and ensure that aggregated information is consistent and accurate.

Further reading

APM Earned Value Specific Interest Group, 2002. *Earned value management: APM guidelines*. Princes Risborough: Association for Project Management.

Association for Project Management, 2010. *The scheduling maturity model. White paper* [online] Available at: www.apm.org.uk/BoK6FurtherReadingg.

Buttrick, R., 2010. The *project workout: the ultimate handbook of project and programme management*. 4th ed. Harlow: FT Prentice-Hall.

Gordon, J. and Lockyer, K., 2005. *Project management and project network techniques*. 7th ed. Harlow: FT Prentice-Hall.

Kerzner, H., 2009. *Project management: a systems approach to planning, scheduling, and controlling*. 10th ed. Hoboken, NJ: Wiley.

Leach, L.P., 2005. *Critical chain project management*. 2nd ed. London: Artech House.

Lester, A., 2007. *Project management, planning and control*. 5th ed. Amsterdam: Elsevier.

Schwindt, C., 2005. *Resource allocation in project management*. Berlin: Springer.

3.3.1 Resource scheduling

Definition
Resource scheduling is a collection of techniques used to calculate the resources required to deliver the work and when they will be required.

General
There are two broad categories of resource – consumable and re-usable. Scheduling these resources ensures:

- efficient and effective utilisation;
- confidence that the schedule is realistic;
- early identification of resource capacity bottlenecks and conflicts.

The resource scheduling process has three steps:

- allocation;
- aggregation;
- scheduling.

Allocation involves identifying what resources are needed to complete the work. In the case of consumable resources it is simply the quantity required. In the case of re-usable resources it is the total effort required and the number of individual resources.

Once time scheduling and resource allocation are complete, the resources can be aggregated on a daily, weekly or monthly basis as appropriate. The aggregated data is usually presented in a histogram that illustrates the fluctuating use of resources against time. In the case of consumable resources a cumulative curve (which usually takes the form of an 's-curve') is also used to show the total amount consumed at any point in time.

Few re-usable resources are limitless, so the time schedule has to be adjusted to take into account the limited availability of resources over time. There are two approaches to reconciling resource limits and time constraints; resource smoothing (or time limited resource scheduling) and resource levelling (or resource limited scheduling).

Resource smoothing is used when the time constraint takes priority. The objective is to complete the work by the required date while avoiding peaks and troughs of resource demand.

A smoothed resource profile will be achieved by delaying some work. This will remove some flexibility from the schedule and its ability to deal with unavoidable delays, but the advantage is usually a more efficient and cost-effective use of resources.

Resource levelling is used when limits on the availability of resources are paramount. It simply answers the question 'With the resources available, when will the work be finished?'

In many situations a mixture of levelling and smoothing may be required. This is particularly true in the programme and portfolio dimensions.

Other factors that can be considered include cost-efficiency measures, such as 'just-in-time' material deliveries; risks affecting resource availability; and the effect of learning curves on performance.

The fully-resourced schedule has to be achievable and have the support of the management team. Unless the team has input into the schedule, this support is likely to be limited at best and withheld at worst.

Resource scheduling may well reveal that the original target, calculated through time scheduling, cannot be achieved. This must be explained to senior management so that expectations can be managed. A fully resourced schedule, taking into account all constraints, will support the case for an extension of time or budget. Without it any case will be less substantial and unlikely to be accepted.

Project

The network analysis models used in time scheduling can be used to perform equally detailed calculations for resource levelling and resource smoothing.

Software packages perform very sophisticated calculations that can result in schedules being significantly changed. The danger with these calculations is that they make cause and effect difficult to determine. For example, if a resource levelling calculation is done that takes limits on five different resources into account and delays the project by a significant amount, it will be virtually impossible to see which resource had the greatest impact.

It should also be borne in mind that concepts such as the critical path and float have little meaning after a resource scheduling calculation has been applied.

An alternative to creating networks based on activity dependencies is to use a technique called critical chain. This method considers the availability of resources and the interdependencies between resources. Once a suitable resource is developed, 'buffers' of spare time are allowed at the end of each path. Monitoring the rate of usage of the buffer time is key in controlling projects based on critical chain.

Programme

The projects and change management activity within a programme will have varied requirements for resource scheduling. The programme management team must decide how resources will be scheduled in each context.

On some projects (or parts of projects) the programme manager may impose time constraints that require the resource schedule to be smoothed. On others, resource constraints may be imposed that require the schedule to be levelled.

The programme and its use of resources are a highly dynamic and complex environment. Successful resource scheduling will depend upon a close working relationship between the programme manager, project managers and business change managers, who all put the needs of the programme ahead of individual projects and change management activity.

A strong programme-support function is vital. Specialist planners (schedulers) will aggregate information from around the programme to show the overall resource profile and assist in evaluating decisions about the allocation of resources and potential bottlenecks.

Portfolio

In general management usage, capacity planning is defined as 'the maximum amount of work that an organisation is capable of completing in a given period '. Capacity planning, in this sense, also applies to portfolios.

In the portfolio domain, resource scheduling is done at a very high level. It is not so much about the timing of resource usage as ensuring that the overall capacity is compatible with the amount of work to be done.

The portfolio practice of categorisation helps break the problem down. Prioritisation shows where resources need to be focused and resource demand is one of the factors taken into account when balancing the portfolio.

A portfolio support function should ensure that projects and programmes produce information that can be aggregated in a consistent and timely manner, enabling the portfolio manager to make informed decisions.

Further reading

APM Earned Value Specific Interest Group, 2002.
Earned value management: APM guidelines. *Princes Risborough:* Association for Project Management.

APM Earned Value Specific Interest Group, 2010.
The earned value management compass. Princes Risborough: Association for Project Management.

Association for Project Management, 2010.
The scheduling maturity model. White paper
[online] Available at: www.apm.org.uk/BoK6FurtherReading.

Cohn, M., 2005.
Agile estimating and planning. London: FT Prentice-Hall.

Gordon, J. and Lockyer, K., 2005.
Project management and project network techniques. 7th ed.
Harlow: FT Prentice-Hall.

Kerzner, H, 2009.
Project management: a systems approach to planning, scheduling, and controlling. 10th ed. Hoboken, NJ: Wiley.

Leach, L.P., 2005.
Critical chain project management. 2nd ed. London: Artech House.

Lester, A., 2007.
Project management, planning and control. 5th ed. Amsterdam: Elsevier.

Lock, D., 2007.
Project management. 9th ed. Aldershot: Gower.

Pennypacker, J.S. and Dye, L.D., 2002.
Managing multiple projects: planning, scheduling and allocating resources for competitive advantage. New York, NY: Marcel Dekker.

Rad, P.F., 2001.
Project estimating and cost management. Vienna, VA: Management Concepts.

Schwindt, C., 2005.
Resource allocation in project management. Berlin: Springer.

3.3.2 Time scheduling

Definition
Time scheduling is a collection of techniques used to develop and present schedules that show when work will be performed.

General
The choice of tools and techniques used to develop a time schedule depends upon the level of detail available about the work that needs to be done.

Where the work is well defined, modelling techniques can be used to show the sequence of working and logical dependencies between each package of work. The resulting model can be used to predict start and finish times, and identify where there is flexibility in the schedule.

If requirements are clear but the means to achieve them is less so, or where the requirements are subject to significant change as the work proceeds, then modelling techniques are less appropriate.

Project
Network analysis can be used where the work is well defined. The analysis process has four stages:

- create a logical model of how the work will be performed;
- estimate activity durations;
- calculate timings for the activities;
- present the results.

Each aspect of the process is considered by the team, using subject-matter experts when appropriate. A schedule agreed by the team is more likely to succeed than one imposed from above.

The logical model is known as a network diagram. This can be drawn in different formats. The common format used by scheduling software is activity-on-node, or precedence networking.

Four types of relationship between two activities can be shown in a precedence network. The most common is 'finish-to-start'. 'Start-to-start' and 'finish-to-finish' are also common. Occasionally a 'start-to-finish' dependency may be appropriate.

Estimating activity durations needs to consider many factors, such as the effort required, the efficiency of resources, physical constraints (e.g. restricted working) etc. Some activities will comprise work that has been done before and is well understood, others will be new or employ innovative methods.

The simplest form of calculation is critical path analysis. This uses one duration estimate that encompasses all the factors. Critical path analysis calculates earliest and latest dates for the performance of each activity and hence the overall duration of the project. It then calculates the amount that individual activities can be delayed without affecting the project finish. This is known as total float. The longest path (or paths) through the network is called the critical path and is made up of activities with the lowest total float.

A refinement of the network diagram is the program evaluation and review technique (PERT). This uses a weighted three-point estimate for each activity's duration in place of a single-point estimate. This enables confidence limits to be applied to the result of the critical path analysis.

The most realistic form of analysis is Monte Carlo. In its simplest form Monte Carlo analysis uses the three-point estimate for activity durations but then performs multiple critical path analyses (typically many hundreds) using different activity durations each time. This results in a statistical model of project duration that can be used to calculate the probability of achieving a specific completion date, or calculating a date by which there is an x% probability of finishing.

In Monte Carlo analysis the concept of a critical path is replaced by the criticality of activities, i.e. how frequently they appear on the critical path in the multiple calculations.

The results of all these techniques are typically presented as a Gantt chart.

The main advantage of a network-based model is that it can be frequently updated with new information and quickly recalculated. This is an ongoing process throughout the project life cycle and uses information about actual progress to predict the eventual project completion.

Earned value management combines time scheduling with cost scheduling. It measures progress in terms of value delivered rather than elapsed time. This is used to provide more accurate predictions of future progress and completion based upon progress to date.

Network analysis is not always the best time-scheduling method. A variety of time-scheduling methods have been developed to suit various technical environments. For example:

- line-of-balance is used on projects that deliver repetitive products (such as a housing estate). This technique is suited to show how resource teams move from product to product rather than the detail of individual activities.
- time is used (typically in IT) on Agile projects. The project is divided into several discrete periods (or 'timeboxes') that typically have durations of between two and six weeks. The work scope and priorities are changed in order to meet the fixed timescale.

- time chainage is used on linear projects such as roads and tunnels. It shows the timing of activities combined with the physical location of the work.

Most project scheduling is performed with the aid of computer software. The many proprietary software packages available enhance the basic scheduling techniques extensively. They also provide considerable choice in the way that schedules are presented and reported. As with all computer software, the quality of information produced is only as good as the quality of the modelling and estimating data input in the first place.

Programme

The overall programme time schedule will reflect all the tranches, projects within each tranche and benefits realisation activity. The scale of programmes often makes it simpler to separate the schedule showing project delivery from the schedule showing benefits realisation.

Dependencies at the programme level will be limited to those that exist between the key deliverables of projects and the relationships between project outputs and dependencies.

Maintaining a detailed network at the programme level is impractical and this kind of modelling is usually restricted to projects. Some specialist software packages allow detailed project schedules to be maintained by the project teams whilst also calculating a high-level programme schedule. This degree of integration can lead to projects having their schedules automatically affected by progress elsewhere. The programme team must ensure that any dependencies between projects and their effects are communicated to the relevant project manager.

Portfolio

The logical dependencies between projects and programmes in a portfolio should be minimal. If there are significant dependencies between two or more projects, for example, the portfolio team should consider whether these should be managed as a single project or as a programme.

Maintaining an overall portfolio schedule can be done using appropriate software. This requires great expertise and the portfolio support function should employ appropriate specialists.

The volume of activity and complexity of interactions between different parts of the portfolio can be difficult to grasp. Automated calculation in these circumstances can lead to a loss of management contact with an ever-changing detailed schedule. Specialist expertise is needed to maintain the integrity of the schedule and to extract and summarise information that supports decisions. These specialists will normally reside within the portfolio support function.

Ideally, these specialists will provide scheduling support to all the component projects and programmes to ensure consistency. They should also provide expert interpretation of the large quantities of information that will be produced.

Further reading

APM Earned Value Specific Interest Group, 2002.
Earned value management: APM guidelines. Princes Risborough: Association for Project Management.

APM Joint Risk and Earned Value Working Group, 2008.
Interfacing risk and earned value management. Princes Risborough: Association for Project Management.

Buttrick, R., 2010.
The project workout: the ultimate handbook of project and programme management. 4th ed. Harlow: FT Prentice-Hall.

Goldratt, E.M., 1997.
Critical chain. Great Barrington, MA: North River Press.

Gordon, J. and Lockyer, K., 2005.
Project management and project network techniques. 7th ed. Harlow: FT Prentice-Hall.

Kerzner, H., 2009.
Project management: a systems approach to planning, scheduling, and controlling. 10th ed. Hoboken, NJ: Wiley.

Lester, A., 2007.
Project management, planning and control. 5th ed. Amsterdam: Elsevier.

Stutzke, R., 2005.
Software project estimation: projects, products, and processes. London: Addison-Wesley.

3.4 Financial and cost management

Definition
Financial management is the process of estimating and justifying costs in order to secure funds, controlling expenditure and evaluating the outcomes.

General
The financial structure of projects, programmes and portfolios takes many different forms but the financial management process is common to all.

The first step is to estimate what the work may cost and the value of its expected benefits. These estimates are made and refined in parallel with other planning processes for establishing the scope of work and estimating schedule, resources and risk.

The balance of cost and benefit is analysed using investment appraisal techniques and documented in the business case. Work is approved if it can be shown not only that the benefits outweigh the costs, but also that the organisation cannot get a better return by investing the same funds elsewhere.

The process of securing funds continues in parallel with these steps. During the early phases of the life cycle, funds may only be committed in principle, pending a more detailed understanding of the work.

As plans are defined in ever greater detail, with increasing levels of confidence, funds will be fully committed and approval given to commence work. Financial governance therefore involves:

- initially: committing funds to the concept phase of the life cycle and reserving funds for the definition phase;
- at the end of the concept phase: committing funds for the definition phase and reserving funds for delivery;
- at the end of the definition phase: committing funds for delivery, or at least the first stage or tranche of work;
- at each review: funds for the next stage or tranche will be dependent upon a viable business case.

As work proceeds, cost-control mechanisms need to be implemented. These will forecast when funds need to be released and track progress of actual expenditure against planned. Funding is reviewed at the end of each stage or tranche of work. Funds are never unlimited and costs have to be balanced against time and scope in accordance with stakeholder requirements.

Financial management arrangements range from the very simple (e.g. a small project within a department) to the highly complex (e.g. a portfolio of international projects and programmes owned by partner organisations), but the principle is always that of ensuring that costs are controlled and exceeded by the value of benefits delivered.

The approach to financial management within a project, programme or portfolio is highly dependent upon the policies, procedures and standards used in the host organisation. These, in turn, are affected by the regulatory and legislative environment.

At the outset, financial procedures must be established that comply with all necessary standards and enable exchange of information with the host organisation's financial systems.

Project

The detail of financial management on a project will depend upon its scale and context.

Small and medium-sized projects will not be able to justify any investment in financial systems unique to the project. They will be serviced by the accounting systems of the host organisation. These are often unable to aggregate and apportion costs according to the project structure, so additional local processing will be necessary.

Larger projects may be able to justify specialist financial systems, ideally linked to the project scheduling systems for progress reporting and forecasting.

In terms of context, a project may be stand-alone or be part of a programme; it may be an internally sponsored and funded project; or a project performed by a contractor on behalf of a client. Financial management must adapt to the context with clear policies for the collection and reporting of cost data.

Programme

Programmes will need to consolidate financial data from three sources: the projects, the business-as-usual activity and the programme management infrastructure.

Finance and accounting policies need to be consistent across the programme. This is a particular challenge where the programme is international, multi-company, or both.

The programme sponsor should pay particular attention to the mechanisms for financial management defined in the definition phase of the programme, and be assured that they are adequate to accurately reflect the financial health of the programme.

Portfolio

If an organisation decides to formalise its management of projects and programmes in a portfolio, it will need to ensure that its systems can capture and provide the type of information required. This may include the ability to build portfolio cost accounts or activity-based costing into the organisation-wide financial systems.

Further reading

Cappels, T., 2003.
Financially focused project management. London: J. Ross.

Goldsmith, L., 2005.
Project management accounting: budgeting, tracking, and reporting costs and profitability. Chichester: Wiley.

3.4.1 Budgeting and cost control

Definition
Budgeting and cost control comprise the estimation of costs, the setting of an agreed budget, and management of actual and forecast costs against that budget.

General
A budget identifies the planned expenditure for a project, programme or portfolio. It is used as a baseline against which the actual expenditure and predicted eventual cost of the work can be reported.

Initial cost estimates can be comparative or parametric. These are refined as the feasibility and desirability of the initiative are investigated and a greater understanding of scope, schedule and resources is developed.

Once approval is given, these refined estimates form the baseline cost. By allocating costs to the activities in a schedule, a profile of expenditure is produced.

The three major components of a P3 budget are:

- the base cost estimate;
- contingency;
- management reserve.

The base cost estimate is made up of known costs such as:

- resourcing (e.g. staff costs or consultants' fees);
- accommodation;
- consumables (e.g. power or IT supplies);
- expenses (e.g. travel and subsistence);
- capital items.

Costs have four possible attributes. They may be direct, indirect, fixed or variable:

- direct costs are exclusive to the project, programme or portfolio; they include resources directly involved in delivering and managing the work;
- indirect costs include overheads and other charges that may be shared out across multiple activities or different departments;
- fixed costs remain the same regardless of how much output is achieved, such as the purchase of an item of plant or machinery;
- variable costs, such as salaries, fluctuate depending on how much resource is used.

Costs may be organised into a cost breakdown structure (CBS) where different levels disaggregate costs into increasingly detailed categories.

Contingency is money set aside for responding to identified risks.

A management reserve covers things that could not have been foreseen, such as changes to the scope of the work or unidentified risks. The more uncertainty there is, the more management reserve is required; so highly innovative work will need a larger management reserve than routine work.

Once the cost estimate, contingency and management reserve are agreed with the sponsor, these become the budget. The simplest way of illustrating the use of the budget against time is the 's-curve'. This shows cumulative expenditure against time and gets its name from its typical shape. This profile of expenditure is used in project financing and funding. It allows a cash flow forecast to be developed, and a drawdown of funds to be agreed.

There should be strict guidelines or rules for managing the contingency and management reserve funds. The P3 manager will have control of the base cost. The sponsor retains control of the contingency and management reserve funds, which may be held as part of broader organisational funds.

Once the work is under way, actual and forecast expenditures are regularly monitored. Costs are tracked either directly by the P3 management team, or indirectly through operational finance systems. Where P3 managers are reliant upon information from operational systems, the information needs to be checked to ensure that costs have been posted correctly.

The normal payment process means that three types of costs must be tracked:

- committed costs – these reflect confirmed orders for future provision of goods and/or services;
- accruals – work partially or fully completed for which payment will be due;
- actual costs – money that has been paid.

The forecast cost is then the sum of commitments, accruals, actual expenditure and an estimate of the cost to complete the remaining work.

A report showing an 's-curve' for the original budget alongside an 's-curve' of actual spend to date, can quickly show how actual expenditure is varying from that originally predicted and form the basis for forecasting.

Actual expenditure inevitably varies from planned expenditure. While the P3 manager will have responsibility for day-to-day management of costs there must be thresholds that require the involvement of the sponsor. These are known as tolerances and, if expenditure is predicted to exceed the tolerances, the manager must escalate this to the sponsor in the form of an issue.

Periodically, the viability of the project, programme or portfolio must be reviewed formally. In the latter stages of the work this review must consider 'sunk costs'.

Sunk costs are actual and committed expenditure that cannot be recovered, plus any additional costs that would be incurred by cancelling contracts. Completing an overspent project or programme may be considered worthwhile if the remaining cost to complete the work is less than the eventual value.

Project

After the initial comparative or parametric estimates, the detailed cost of a project will be estimated bottom-up using the work breakdown structure (WBS).

By classifying costs in accordance with the WBS, CBS and organisational breakdown structure (OBS), they can be reported in any combination of cost type, resource type and part of the project. Estimates may be drawn from internal costs (such as salaries) or external costs (such as provider quotations); they may be drawn from previous experience of similar projects or be more speculative where the work is innovative. Where cost estimates are difficult to pin down, three-point estimates of optimistic, pessimistic and most likely costs allow a statistical analysis of the overall project cost.

The baseline cost can be used as the basis for earned value management (EVM). This assumes that the cost of performing the work constitutes its value. The value of work performed at any point can then be compared to the actual cost of performing it and the value of work planned to have been performed at that point. The type of work in a project is usually in a narrow range. This enables earned value management to make predictions about future performance based on performance to date more accurately than techniques such as critical path analysis.

Many internal resources on a project will not be fully dedicated to the project. They may be part of a matrix organisation where their time is split between business-as-usual and multiple projects. In this situation, it is important to have a system of cost allocation that accurately reflects the costs consumed by the project.

Programme

Programmes frequently cut across operational departments and may be funded from different sources. The programme manager must understand how the budget is funded so that cost reports can be fed back to the appropriate stakeholders. Within a diverse programme there may be innovative projects and routine projects. As well as projects, costs will be incurred in business-as-usual areas. The estimating accuracy across the programme will also vary widely. At any point in time the programme will include projects that are well defined and accurately costed, projects that are in the future and yet to be defined, benefits realisation work that is clearly part of the programme, and business-as-usual work that is arguably part of the programme.

This variation makes it difficult to provide an overall picture of the programme's financial position. The financial performance of a programme cannot easily be represented as a simple 's-curve' and suitable reporting mechanisms will have to be set out and agreed with stakeholders.

A programme support function will need to establish clear cost accounting procedures that are adhered to by all projects and benefits realisation work. Business change managers will need to be clear on business-as-usual costs that can be allocated to the programme.

Portfolio

Portfolios are aligned to corporate financial cycles. Budgets for portfolios are less concerned with the cost of delivering a specific result, and more to do with what can be delivered within a defined budget.

The prioritisation and balancing phases of the portfolio life cycle depend upon a good understanding of the costs of the component projects and programmes. One of the most common causes of cost control problems is over-optimism about what can be delivered within the available budget.

It is unlikely that cost variance reporting will be appropriate for the portfolio as a whole, but it may be appropriate for categories of project and programme within the portfolio.

The portfolio management team is responsible for setting standards of cost estimating, accounting and reporting across all the component aspects of the portfolio so that sound decisions can be made.

Further reading

APM Earned Value Specific Interest Group, 2002. *Earned value management: APM guidelines*. Princes Risborough: Association for Project Management.

APM Earned Value Specific Interest Group, 2010. *The earned value management compass*. Princes Risborough: Association for Project Management.

Brooks, F.P., 1995. *The mythical man month and other essays on software engineering*. 2nd ed. White Plains, NY: Addison-Wesley.

Cappels, T., 2003. *Financially focused project management*. London: J. Ross.

Goldsmith, L., 2005. *Project management accounting: budgeting, tracking, and reporting costs and profitability*. Chichester: Wiley.

Rad, P.F., 2001. *Project estimating and cost management*. Vienna, VA: Management Concepts.

Stenzel, C. and Stenzel, J., 2002. *Essentials of cost management*. Hoboken, NJ: Wiley.

Taylor, J.C., 2005. *Project cost estimating tools, techniques and perspectives*. Boca, FL: St Lucie Press.

3.4.2 Funding

Definition

Funding is the means by which the capital required to undertake a project, programme or portfolio is secured and then made available as required.

General

Funding can be from internal or external sources or a combination of both. The scale of funding may be as simple as allocation of funds from a single departmental budget, to complex, international financing of a joint venture. In some cases the work may be expected to be self-funding, with revenues generated from earlier stages of work providing funds to deliver the later stages.

Internal funding comes from reserves already allocated to operational expenditure (OPEX) or capital expenditure (CAPEX). In the normal business planning cycle, internal funds are distributed across different subsidiary, regional or departmental budgets. A project, programme or portfolio can be funded from one or more of these budgets.

The total internal funding for organisational initiatives is limited, so conditions are typically attached to when funds can be committed. An organisation's business planning cycle, most notably its financial year and quarters, is likely to be a major factor in determining when funds are available.

Internal funds will often come from one or more budgets, each with its own budget holder. The budget holders will contribute funds and delegate management to the sponsor. They are likely to be the eventual recipients of the benefits created by the work.

Internal funding for major, vision-led, organisational change may bypass departmental budgets and come direct from the executive board.

External funding of projects and programmes takes many forms. This includes loans in the form of overdrafts or capital, funds from shareholders through rights issues, venture capital or grants.

P3 managers and sponsors must be fully aware of the terms and conditions associated with external funding. The external funders may not be involved in the benefits of the work in any way; they may simply supply the money.

Whether internal or external, recipients of benefits or not, funders must be treated as key stakeholders and managed accordingly.

For major international initiatives other factors also come into play including credit guarantees, currency fluctuations and the complexity of international funding.

Project

Where a project is funded from departmental budgets, the sponsor of the project may well be the person who owns that budget. If a larger project spans multiple-departmental budgets, it is the sponsor's responsibility to work with budget holders to secure funds for the project.

Where a project is performed by a contracting organisation on behalf of a client organisation, regular valuations will be performed to calculate stage payments. These payments from the client organisation are the contractor's main source of funding. However, there will be a time delay between expenditure on resources and payment from the client. The contractor will need to secure funds to cover the cash flow difference.

In the UK public sector, there are a number of funding arrangements that have been put in place by government to form partnerships with the private sector for major projects. These include the private finance initiative (PFI), public private partnership (PPP) and build, own, operate and transfer (BOOT).

PFI is principally a procurement tool, designed to harness private sector management, expertise and resources in the delivery of public services, while reducing the impact on public sector borrowing. PPP is an ownership structure in which the government has an equity stake in the asset. BOOT can be applied to a private sector initiative as well as a public-private sectors one. In a BOOT project, one organisation is given a concession from the commissioning organisation to fund, build, operate and eventually transfer a facility.

As the close of a project is reached, the project manager must ensure that all financial commitments have been met and any unspent funds are identified to the relevant authority.

Programme

The scale of programmes means that they are very likely to either rely on multiple-internal budgets, or be directly funded from executive board level. If funds are provided from multiple-internal budgets, the sponsor must be aware of the budgeting cycle and the possibility that changes in departmental budgets can affect the funding of the programme.

Once the sponsor has secured funding for the programme, the programme management team is responsible for funding the component projects and change management activity. It must always be aware that it is really funding the delivery of benefits; the projects are simply the means of creating the outputs that enable the benefits to be realised.

The relationship between projects and benefits must be fully understood to ensure that funds are allocated and re-allocated in accordance with the benefits they create. This may involve moving funds between projects, re-scoping projects or even their cancellation in order to use funds more effectively.

Portfolio

An organisational-level portfolio is funded as part of the business planning cycle. Ideally, the objectives of the portfolio will be delivered within the same time frame. If not, the portfolio runs the risk of having its funding changed in the next business planning cycle and with it the continued funding of projects and programmes. The same principle is true of a departmental portfolio but the timescale is likely to be annual.

The way in which a portfolio is categorised, prioritised and balanced will, to a large degree, depend upon how it is funded. For example, there may be levels of uncertainty regarding future availability of funding. Long-term secured funds will be committed to the longer, high-priority programmes, while short-term funds will be matched to shorter-term projects or smaller programmes.

Further reading

APM Joint Risk and Earned Value Working Group, 2008.
Interfacing risk and earned value management. Princes Risborough: Association for Project Management.

Euromoney Institutional Investor, 2003.
Project finance: the guide to value and risk management in PPP projects.
London: Euromoney Institutional Investor.

Gatti, S., 2007.
Project finance in theory and practice: designing, structuring, and financing private and public projects. London: Academic Press.

Grimsey, D. and Lewis, M.K., 2007.
Public private partnerships: the worldwide revolution in infrastructure provision and project finance. Cheltenham: Edward Elgar.

Khan, F. and Parra, R., 2003.
Financing large projects: using project finance techniques and practices.
Hong Kong: Person Education Asia.

Yescombe, E., 2002.
Principles of project finance. London: Academic Press.

Yescombe, E., 2007.
Public-private partnerships: principles of policy and finance.
Oxford: Butterworth-Heinemann.

3.4.3 Investment appraisal

Definition
Investment appraisal is a collection of techniques used to identify the attractiveness of an investment.

General
The purpose of investment appraisal is to assess the viability of project, programme or portfolio decisions and the value they generate. In the context of a business case, the primary objective of investment appraisal is to place a value on benefits so that the costs are justified.

There are many factors that can form part of an appraisal. These include:

■ financial – this is the most commonly assessed factor;
■ legal – the value of an investment may be in it enabling an organisation to meet current or future legislation;
■ environmental – the impact of the work on the environment is increasingly a factor when considering an investment;
■ social – for charitable organisations, return on investment could be measured in terms of 'quality of life' or even 'lives saved';
■ operational – benefits may be expressed in terms of 'increased customer satisfaction', 'higher staff morale' or 'competitive advantage';
■ risk – all organisations are subject to business and operational risk. An investment decision may be justified because it reduces risk.

A financial appraisal is the most easily quantifiable approach but it can only be applied to benefits that produce financial returns.

The simplest financial appraisal technique is the payback method. The payback period is the time it takes for net cash inflow to equal the cash investment. This is a relatively crude assessment and is often used simply as an initial screening process.

A better way of comparing alternative investments is the accounting rate of return (ARR) which expresses the 'profit' as a percentage of the costs. However, this has the disadvantage of not taking into account the timing of income and expenditure. This makes a significant difference on all but the shortest and most capital-intensive of projects.

In most cases, discounted cash flow techniques such as net present value (NPV) or internal rate of return (IRR) are appropriate to evaluate the value of benefits and alternative ways of delivering them. NPV calculates the present value of cash flows associated with an investment; the higher the NPV the better. This calculation uses a discount rate to show how the value of money decreases with time. The discount rate that gives an investment an NPV value of zero is called the IRR. NPV and IRR can be compared for a number of options.

Appraisal of capital-intensive projects and programmes should take into account the whole-life costs across the complete product life cycle as there may be significant termination costs. In the case of the public sector, where income is usually zero, it is common practice to identify the option with the lowest whole-life cost as the option that offers the best value for money.

The appraisal on less tangible and non-financial factors is more subjective. In some cases, a financial value may be calculated by applying a series of assumptions. For example, work that improved staff morale may lead to lower staff turnover and reduce recruitment costs. A financial appraisal of this benefit would have to include assumptions about the numerical impact of increased morale on staff turnover and the estimated costs of recruitment.

Where benefits cannot be quantified then scoring methods may be used to compare the subjective value of benefits.

Project

Stand-alone projects will use investment appraisal to compare alternative approaches to achieving the required benefits. Wherever possible, the project should use techniques that are the organisational, programme or portfolio standard approach.

Where a project is part of a programme, the initial investment appraisal may be performed by the programme management team. That does not exempt the project management team from being familiar with the content of the appraisal or the techniques used to perform it. It will still be responsible for keeping the business case up to date and this will involve repeating the investment calculations to account for changing circumstances.

Where a project is undertaken by a contracting organisation, the financial appraisal is relatively straightforward as it will simply be a comparison of costs with the fee paid by the client, probably using a discounted cash flow technique.

Programme

Programmes are usually defined to bring about organisational change. This inevitably gives rise to a higher proportion of intangible and non-financial benefits being included in the business case. Commercial programmes must be careful not to be overly dependent on non-financial benefits, as anything can be justified through subjective views of value.

The programme management team must set out standards for the appraisal of the component projects and their associated benefits. Consistent and compatible

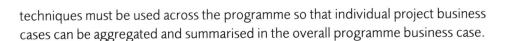

techniques must be used across the programme so that individual project business cases can be aggregated and summarised in the overall programme business case.

Portfolio

In the definition phase of a portfolio there may be many ideas and suggestions for projects and programmes to meet the strategic objectives. The portfolio management team must establish a system for capturing and screening these ideas.

This is where broad-brush techniques such as payback may be used. A criterion may be set that requires payback within the financial planning cycle. Any projects or programmes that do not provide payback in that period are discarded. As the higher-potential ideas are captured, they will be subject to more detailed, analytical techniques.

The prioritisation and balancing phases of the portfolio will rely heavily on how investment appraisal has built the business cases of the component projects and programmes. It is essential that the portfolio management team establishes standard methods and consistent approaches across the portfolio to ensure reliable decision-making. The team should also provide specialist advice and guidance on the use of appraisal techniques to all project and programme teams.

The portfolio management team must also ensure that investment appraisals consider potential investments in the context of the existing and planned projects and programmes. For example, to identify opportunities for reuse of components and avoid double counting of benefits.

Further reading

HM Treasury, 2003.
The green book. [online] Available at: www.apm.org.uk/BoK6FurtherReading.

Rogers, M., 2001.
Engineering project appraisal. Oxford: Blackwell Science.

3.5 **Risk management**

Definition
Risk management is a process that allows individual risk events and overall risk to be understood and managed proactively, optimising success by minimising threats and maximising opportunities.

General
All projects, programmes and portfolios are inherently risky because they are unique, constrained, based on assumptions, performed by people and subject to external influences. Risks can affect the achievement of objectives either positively or negatively. Risk includes both opportunities and threats, and both should be managed through the risk management process.

Risk is defined at two levels for projects, programmes and portfolios. At the detailed level, an individual risk is defined as 'an uncertain event or set of circumstances that, should it occur, will have an effect on achievement of one or more objectives'. In addition, at the higher level of the project, programme or portfolio, overall risk is defined as 'exposure of stakeholders to the consequences of variation in outcome' arising from an accumulation of individual risks together with other sources of uncertainty.

The high-level process, as illustrated in figure 3.12 starts with an initiation step that defines the scope and objectives of risk management. A key output from the initiation step is the risk management plan, which details how risk will be managed throughout the life cycle.

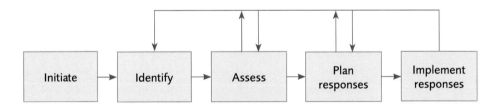

Figure 3.12: Risk management process

Risks are then identified and documented in the risk register. The relative significance of identified risks is assessed using qualitative techniques to enable them to be prioritised for further attention. Quantitative risk analysis may also be used to determine the combined effect of risks on objectives.

The process continues with risk response planning, aiming to avoid, reduce, transfer or accept threats as well as exploit, enhance, share or reject opportunities, with contingency (time, cost, resources and course of action) for risks which cannot be managed proactively. The final step is the implementation of agreed responses.

The whole process is iterative. For example, assessment or response planning can lead to the identification of further risks; planning and implementing responses can trigger a need for further analysis, and so on.

It is also important to identify and manage behavioural influences on the risk process, both individual and group, since these can have a significant impact on risk management effectiveness.

Risk management at project, programme or portfolio level must not be conducted in isolation and must interface with the organisation. Risks at project level may need escalation to programme and portfolio. Risks can also be delegated from higher levels to lower levels.

In addition, P3 risk management must contribute, as appropriate, to both business risk assessments and organisational governance requirements. The P3 manager must be aware of risks that have an effect outside their scope of responsibility, e.g. those that could affect the organisation's reputation.

The management of general health and safety risks is usually excluded from P3 risk management, as the management of these risks is traditionally handled by a separate function within the organisation.

Project

Risk management at project level is most often focused on individual risks that, should they occur, will affect the project's objectives. It is, however, also important for the project manager to understand the overall risk exposure of the project, so that this can be reported to the project sponsor and other stakeholders.

Risk management must be closely aligned to schedule management. Cost, time and resource estimates should always take risks into account.

The project manager is accountable for ensuring that risk management takes place. Depending on the size and complexity of the project, a specialist risk manager may be appointed to oversee and facilitate the risk management process.

Programme

The programme will establish a common framework and standards for risk management across the programme. This will enable comparison of risk, reduce the time taken to initiate management processes at project level, and help identify interdependencies between risks across the programme. The common framework will be set out in the programme risk management plan.

Programme risk management is made up of two distinct areas of focus:

- project risk escalation and aggregation;
- wider business risk and risks to benefit achievement.

Programme risk management addresses any individual risks at project level that, if realised, will have a wider impact. Project risks that cannot be effectively managed within projects and within contingency are escalated to the programme for attention and/or action. In addition, related or common risks within individual projects may combine or aggregate to have an effect at programme level, in which case they also need to be escalated.

Programme risk management also considers any risks delegated from the portfolio or strategic level, as well as risks arising directly at the level of the programme itself. Programme risks are likely to focus on prioritisation of programme components, allocation of resources, interfaces and interactions between programme components, the ability to deliver change management activities within the programme, and cumulative risks arising from the combined impact of the project risks.

Portfolio

Risks at portfolio level are often of such scale that they may have significant impact on the ability of the organisation to operate. Portfolio risk management will focus on two areas:

- risks escalated from projects or programmes and from areas of day-to-day business;
- risks that impact upon the objectives of the portfolio and the host organisation.

Project and programme risks that cannot be effectively managed at their originating level may be escalated to the portfolio for responses unavailable at project or programme level.

The portfolio will establish common frameworks and standards for risk management, which will be cascaded to projects and programmes to ensure a common approach and reporting structure. This enables effective comparison of risk, reduces the time taken in initiating risk management processes, and assists with identification of potential conflict in selected responses across the portfolio.

The consideration of risk efficiency is of particular importance to portfolio risk management. The principles of risk efficiency have been established in financial portfolios for many years. They are equally relevant to portfolios of projects and programmes. Ensuring that the portfolio does not expose an organisation to too much risk and is efficient is an important function in the 'balance' phase of the portfolio life cycle.

Further reading

APM Joint Risk and Earned Value Working Group, 2008.
Interfacing risk and earned value management. Princes Risborough: Association for Project Management.

Association for Project Management, 2004.
Project risk analysis and management (PRAM) guide. 2nd ed. Princes Risborough: Association for Project Management.

British Standards Institution, 2011.
BS 31100:2011 risk management – code of practice and guidance for the implementation of BS ISO 31000.
[online] Available at: www.apm.org.uk/BoK6FurtherReading.

British Standards Institution, 2011. BS 31100:2011 risk management - code of practice and guidance for the implementation of BS ISO 31000. London: BSI.

Chapman, C.B. and Ward, S.C., 2003.
Project risk management: processes, techniques and insights. 2nd ed. Chichester: Wiley.

Hillson D.A., 2003.
Effective opportunity management for projects: exploiting positive risk. New York, NY: Marcel Dekker.

International Organization for Standardization, 2009.
ISO 31000:2009 risk management - principles and guidelines.
[online] Available at: www.apm.org.uk/BoK6FurtherReading.

International Organization for Standardization, 2009. ISO 31000:2009 risk management - principles and guidelines. Geneva: ISO.

3.5.1 Risk context

Definition

The risk context describes the institutional and individual environment, attitudes and behaviours that affect the way risk arises and the way it should be managed.

General

The risk context is a complex system. It is affected by individuals, groups (such as the project management team), stakeholders, host organisations, clients and the broad external environment.

Fundamental to understanding the context are the concepts of risk attitude and risk appetite.

Risk attitude is an individual's or group's natural disposition towards uncertainty and is influenced by their perception of risk. Perception is itself influenced by many factors, including conscious and subconscious reactions to risk. Risk attitude will affect the way people develop responses to risk and the way they react if a risk event occurs.

The risk attitude of a group or individual is often described in one of three ways:

- risk averse, where risk is avoided;
- risk seeking, where risk is actively sought;
- risk neutral, where risk is neither actively sought nor avoided.

A risk averse attitude may be useful in some situations (e.g. local government) but detrimental in others (e.g. an entrepreneurial, technology start-up company). Conversely, risk seeking is a positive attribute in some situations but unsuitable in others.

Understanding risk attitude can help P3 managers by giving insight into why some situations are considered more risky than others, and why individuals or groups behave in certain ways when confronted with risk.

Risk appetite is the amount of risk an individual, group or organisation is prepared to take in order to achieve their objectives to take risk in a given situation, influenced by their propensity to take risk and/or the organisational risk culture.

A P3 manager needs to understand the risk appetite of the stakeholders. In the definition phase of a life cycle the development of a solution to meet requirements will be heavily influenced by the stakeholders' risk appetite. Some ways of meeting requirements may be delivered quickly or produce high returns but also involve high levels of risk. These would be acceptable to risk-seeking stakeholders but not to those who are risk averse.

The P3 manager also needs to understand the risk attitude of the team members and ensure that they are managed in a way that is compatible with the stakeholders' risk appetite.

Project

Many projects will derive their risk appetite from their host programme, portfolio or organisation. The project manager must understand the context in which the project is to be delivered and handle project risk accordingly.

Where a project involves multiple organisations, the project manager will need to balance the needs of different groups of stakeholders. For example, where a project is being delivered by a contractor on behalf of a client, there may be different appetites for risk. The contractor may be risk averse to protect profit on the contract, whereas the client may be risk seeking if there are opportunities to increase the value of the project's output.

Programme

The programme management team must ensure that the acceptable level of risk for the programme is reflected in the management of project risk. This does not mean that every project will need to have the same risk appetite, but the projects must be structured and balanced with the overall acceptable level of risk in mind.

Portfolio

In delivering an organisation's strategic objectives, a portfolio will take on the same risk appetite as the host organisation. The organisation's risk appetite may allow for some high-risk ventures to be initiated, provided they are balanced by low-risk ventures.

Techniques such as risk efficiency are useful in ensuring that the overall risk of a portfolio does not exceed an organisation's appetite for risk.

Further reading

Association for Project Management, 2004. *Project risk analysis and management (PRAM) guide*. 2nd ed. Princes Risborough: Association for Project Management.

Chapman, C.B. and Ward, S.C., 2003. *Project risk management: processes, techniques and insights*. 2nd ed. Chichester: Wiley.

Hillson, D.A., 2003. *Effective opportunity management for projects: exploiting positive risk*. New York, NY: Marcel Dekker.

Hillson, D.A. and Murray-Webster, R., 2005. *Understanding and managing risk attitude*. Aldershot: Gower.

Institute of Risk Management National Forum for Risk Management in the Public Sector (ALARM) and Association of Insurance and Risk Managers (AIRMIC), 2002. *A risk management standard*.
[online] Available at:www.apm.org.uk/BoK6FurtherReading.

3.5.2 Risk techniques

Definition
Risk management techniques are used to identify, assess and plan responses to individual risks and overall risk.

General
There are numerous different techniques available to assist in risk management and it is important to ensure that the correct techniques are selected and used. None of these are totally unique to P3 management; what is unique is the context in which they are employed.

Identification techniques draw on various sources of information. Identification of risks from previous projects, programmes and portfolios involves looking at lessons learned reports and risk registers. In more mature organisations these may have been collated and structured in the form of checklists and prompt lists. A P3 manager can then use these lists as an aide memoire to instigate identification of risks before moving on to other techniques.

Identifying risks through stakeholders and team members can be on a one-to-one basis or in groups. Individuals with specific knowledge or expertise may be interviewed. Groups can be brought together for brainstorming sessions or coordinated through a 'Delphi' process.

Since risk is inherent in all aspects of P3 management, risks will be revealed through many other P3 management processes. Stakeholder management will identify risks associated with stakeholders, solutions development will highlight technical risks, schedule management will identify risks with delivery methods, and so on. Risk identification is a component of all P3 management processes.

Techniques for assessing risks fall into two categories; qualitative and quantitative.

Qualitative risk assessment focuses on individual risks and is based on educated opinion and expert judgement. Qualitative techniques include probability and impact assessment, influence diagrams and expected value calculations. Quantitative risk assessment focuses on overall risk and is based on more numerical approaches. Typical quantitative techniques include Monte Carlo analysis, decision trees and sensitivity analysis.

Planned responses to risks vary according to whether the risk is a threat or an opportunity. The possible responses to threats are to avoid, reduce, transfer or accept them. These responses act differently on the probability that a risk will occur and the impact it will have on objectives. If the risk is an opportunity, the possible responses are to exploit, enhance, share or reject it. The two sets of responses are fundamentally the same, but tailored to minimise the detrimental effect of a threat or maximise the beneficial effect of an opportunity.

There is no one size fits all approach to the selection of techniques and they will be of most value when selected to match the context in which they are deployed. The cost, benefits and potential difficulties of using particular techniques should be understood. For risk management to be successful, a complementary and cost-effective suite of techniques should be chosen for each project, programme or portfolio.

Project

All the techniques are applicable to projects, but smaller projects can usually only justify the simpler techniques with a lower management overhead.

Large or complex projects will need to apply the more sophisticated techniques. The resources needed to implement these must be included in the risk management plan and the cost implications included in the budget.

Programme

The programme risk management plan will outline the use of techniques in its component projects. It is vitally important for the programme to set guidelines to ensure consistency. Without consistency, it is difficult to aggregate risk from the component projects and business-as-usual to get a value for the overall risk of the programme.

All identification and response techniques are applicable across the programme, but it is impractical to apply some quantitative assessment techniques, e.g. Monte Carlo analysis, at the programme level.

Portfolio

Portfolios will establish common guidelines for using risk management techniques but are also able to develop long-term attitudes and behaviour that ensure that they are used appropriately.

Portfolios are directly affected by the external environment. They need to identify risks from the broadest range of sources and may utilise techniques such as PESTLE to assess the external sources of risk.

The risk efficiency technique has been established in financial portfolios for many years. The term 'balanced portfolio' applies equally well to a portfolio of projects and programmes as it does to stocks, shares and other investments. This is an important technique during the 'balance' phase of the portfolio life cycle.

Further reading

Association for Project Management, 2004.
Project risk analysis and management (PRAM) guide. 2nd ed. Princes Risborough: Association for Project Management.

Chapman, C.B. and Ward, S.C., 2003.
Project risk management: processes, techniques and insights. 2nd ed. Chichester: Wiley.

Hillson, D.A., 2003.
Effective opportunity management for projects: exploiting positive risk. New York, NY: Marcel Dekker.

Hillson, D.A. and Murray-Webster, R., 2005.
Understanding and managing risk attitude. Aldershot: Gower.

Institute of Risk Management National Forum for Risk Management in the Public Sector (ALARM) and Association of Insurance and Risk Managers (AIRMIC), 2002.
A risk management standard.
[online] Available at: www.apm.org.uk/BoK6FurtherReading.

3.6 Quality management

Definition

Quality management is a discipline for ensuring that outputs, benefits, and the processes by which they are delivered, meet stakeholder requirements and are fit for purpose.

General

Quality management has four components; quality planning, quality assurance, quality control and continual improvement. These include procedures, tools and techniques that are used to ensure that the outputs and benefits meet customer requirements.

The first component, quality planning, involves the preparation of a quality management plan that describes the processes and metrics that will be used. The quality management plan needs to be agreed with relevant stakeholders to ensure that their expectations for quality are correctly identified. The processes described in the quality management plan should conform to the processes, culture and values of the host organisation.

Quality assurance provides confidence to the host organisation that its projects, programmes and portfolios are being well managed. It validates the consistent use of procedures and standards, and ensures that staff have the correct knowledge, skills and attitudes to fulfil their project roles and responsibilities in a competent manner. Quality assurance must be independent of the project, programme or portfolio to which it applies.

The next component, quality control, consists of inspection, testing and measurement. It verifies that the deliverables conform to specification, are fit for purpose and meet stakeholder expectations.

Quality control activities determine whether acceptance criteria have, or have not, been met. For this to be effective, specifications must be under strict configuration control. It is possible that, once agreed, the specification may need to be modified. Commonly this is to accommodate change requests or issues, while maintaining acceptable time and cost constraints. Any consequent changes to acceptance criteria should be approved and communicated.

The last component, continual improvement, is the generic term used by organisations to describe how information provided by quality assurance and quality control processes is used to drive improvements in efficiency and effectiveness. A P3 maturity model provides a framework against which continual improvement can be initiated and embedded in the organisation.

Project

Projects that are part of a programme may well have much of the quality management plan developed at programme level to ensure that standards are consistent with the rest of the programme. Stand-alone projects need to develop their own quality management plans, either from scratch or by adapting those from other similar projects. This may seem to be an administrative burden at the beginning of smaller projects, but is always worthwhile in the end.

Projects deliver tangible outputs that are subject to many forms of quality control, depending upon the technical nature of the work and codes affecting particular industries. Examples of inspecting deliverables include crushing samples of concrete used in the foundations of a building; x-raying welds in a ship's hull; and following the test script for a new piece of software.

Inspection produces data and tools such as scatter diagrams, control charts, flowcharts and cause and effect diagrams, all of which help to understand the quality of work and how it may be improved.

The main contribution to continual improvement that can be made within the timescale of a project is through lessons learned. Existing lessons learned should be consulted at the beginning of every project, and any relevant lessons used in the preparation of the project documentation. At the end of every project, the lessons learned should be documented as part of the post-project review and fed back into the knowledge database.

Programme

The responsibility of the programme management team is to develop a quality management plan that encompasses the varied contexts and technical requirements contained within the programme. This sets the standards for the project quality management plans and also acts as a plan for quality in the benefits realisation parts of the programme.

A comprehensive quality management plan at programme level can greatly reduce the effort involved in preparing project-level quality management plans.

Quality control of outputs is mainly handled at project level, but the programme may get involved where an output from one project is an input to another, or where additional inspection is needed when outputs from two or more projects are brought together.

The programme is responsible for quality control of benefits. This is a complex task since the acceptance criteria of a benefit may cover subjective as well as measurable factors but benefits should be defined in measurable terms so that quality control can be applied.

The typical scale of programmes means that they have a very useful role to play in continual improvement. Programme assurance will ensure that projects do take existing lessons learned into account and then capture their own lessons for addition to the knowledge database.

Portfolio

The very nature of a portfolio means that it is unlikely to need a portfolio quality management plan. Quality management for the portfolio should be indistinguishable from the quality management policies of the host organisation as a whole.

It may be necessary for the portfolio management team to provide guidance on the application of general policies or perhaps augment them where the portfolio creates special requirements.

The portfolio is responsible for delivering strategic objectives. These may be expressed in very broad terms resulting in difficulty in applying quality control. When establishing the scope of a portfolio, attention should be given to defining acceptance criteria for strategic objectives so that they can be quality controlled.

Continual improvement is very much a concern at portfolio level. The portfolio management team needs to ensure that the management of projects and programmes becomes more effective and efficient with the passage of time.

Further reading

APM Governance of Project Management Specific Interest Group, 2005.
Directing change: a guide to governance of project management. 2nd ed. Princes Risborough: Association for Project Management.

Bartlett, J., 2005.
Right first and every time: managing quality in projects and programmes. Hook: Project Manager Today Publications.

British Standards Institution, 2000.
BS EN ISO 9000:2000 quality management systems. Fundamentals and vocabulary. London: British Standards Institution.

British Standards Institution, 2000.
BS EN ISO 9004:2000 quality management systems. Guidelines for performance improvements. London: British Standards Institution.

British Standards Institution, 2003.
BS EN ISO 10006:2003 quality management systems. Guidelines for quality management in projects. London: British Standards Institution

British Standards Institution, 2008.
BS EN ISO 9001:2008 quality management systems. Requirements. London: BSI

Rose, K., 2005. *Project quality management: why, what and how*. London: J. Ross.

3.6.1 P3 Assurance

Definition

P3 assurance is the process of providing confidence to stakeholders that projects, programmes and portfolios will achieve their scope, time, cost and quality objectives, and realise their benefits.

General

The sponsor is responsible for P3 assurance, which differs from quality assurance in that it is performed within the P3 organisation. It must be independent of those directly involved in the delivery of work. This independence can be achieved in a number of ways including, for example, using individuals external to the delivery team, or merely by regular and formal reporting of agreed information in a manner that cannot be influenced by the delivery team. Assurance makes recommendations but not decisions, although it forms a sound basis upon which decisions are taken.

Assurance will often be risk-based, with the riskiest aspects of the work being subject to the most rigorous assurance processes. In this context, the term 'risk' relates to the management environment, rather than the delivery risks that would appear in a P3 risk register.

These risks may, for example, relate to the experience of a project manager, or the ability of the host organisation's systems to provide the necessary financial data. The risk assessment which drives this assurance needs to take into account contextual and environmental risks, as well as the possibility of unforeseen and emergent risks.

More complex projects, programmes and portfolios typically need a suite of assurance processes. This ensures that all aspects are adequately covered, e.g. security, regulatory compliance, governance processes.

In these environments a number of different assurance providers may be needed, each of which will have their own processes and defined scope designed to meet the needs of one group of stakeholders. It is possible for the total assurance burden to become onerous in these circumstances. This in itself presents a risk of progress being jeopardised by the very process that is supposed to increase confidence in the achievement of the deliverables.

When there are a number of assurance providers, the sponsor must get them to work in a coordinated manner, sharing information where possible and ensuring that all aspects are covered. This approach is known as integrated assurance.

The intended approach to P3 assurance, the resources required and scheduled reviews are all set out in the quality management plan. Since it is the sponsor's responsibility to ensure that independent project assurance is implemented, the project assurance part of the quality management plan has to be prepared by the sponsor or delegated to someone not involved in delivery.

Assurance will involve reviews and audits but it should not be reduced to a simple inspection of management processes. The resources responsible for assurance should be capable of providing advice, guidance and support in the implementation of governance processes.

Typically, assurance resources will come from the support function, provided that they are independent from the delivery of the project, programme or portfolio. It is the sponsor's responsibility to use the results of the assurance process to address any failings in the management of the project and instil confidence in the project amongst its stakeholders.

Project

Where the project is part of a programme or portfolio, the assurance reviews and audits will be conducted by the programme or portfolio support function. Where the project is stand-alone, the sponsor must secure resources from outside the project to provide assurance.

Programme

Within a programme there are two levels of assurance: assurance of the projects and benefits realisation activities; and assurance of the programme management process.

The programme manager often fulfils the role of sponsor for the component projects and, in this position, has responsibility for project assurance, while remaining independent from programme assurance. This will require the programme sponsor to plan assurance using separate resources for project and programme-level assurance.

Portfolio

At the portfolio level, arrangements within projects and programmes interface with the host organisation's assurance function. The host organisation will typically have mandated assurance functions. It is usually the responsibility of those in charge of these business-wide functions to ensure that the business has the assurance it needs.

Portfolio assurance needs to flow to the organisation's board as it provides a critical link between assurance and organisational governance. Usually, the organisation's audit committee has a general duty for ensuring that the board has the assurance that it needs. The audit committee, therefore, has a key assurance role to play within portfolio management.

Further reading

APM Governance of Project Management Specific Interest Group, 2005.
Directing change: a guide to governance of project management. 2ⁿᵈ ed.
Princes Risborough: Association for Project Management.

Bartlett, J., 2005.
Right first and every time: managing quality in projects and programmes. Hook:
Project Manager Today Publications.

British Standards Institution, 2000.
BS EN ISO 9000:2000 quality management systems. Fundamentals and vocabulary.
London: British Standards Institution.

British Standards Institution, 2000.
BS EN ISO 9004:2000 quality management systems. Guidelines for performance improvements. London: British Standards Institution.

British Standards Institution, 2003.
BS EN ISO 10006:2003 quality management systems. Guidelines for quality management in projects. London: BSI.

British Standards Institution, 2008.
BS EN ISO 9001:2008 Quality management systems. Requirements. London: BSI.

Reiss, G. et al., 2006.
The Gower handbook of programme management. London: Gower.

Rose, K., 2005.
Project quality management: why, what and how. London: J. Ross.

3.6.2 Reviews

Definition
A review is a critical evaluation of a deliverable, business case or P3 management process.

General
Reviews are one of the principle mechanisms by which the quality of deliverables, performance of the management process and the on-going viability of the work are assured.

They may take many forms and occur at many different levels within the P3 environment, but essentially investigate one of three aspects of a project, programme or portfolio:

- deliverables: a review can be a procedure for quality control of products delivered by a project or programme;
- the business case: the continued desirability, viability and achievability of the work should be reviewed at set points in the life cycle. This type of review can result in premature closure of projects and programmes;
- management processes: in this instance a review is part of P3 assurance to check that the work is being well managed.

Reviews can be triggered by events (e.g. the delivery of a product or completion of a stage) or by the passage of time (e.g. quarterly or six-monthly reviews). Initial plans and budgets should provide for reviews to be undertaken as necessary.

The frequency, conduct and scheduling of reviews is set out in the quality management plan. The plan must ensure that reviews are appropriate in terms of depth and breadth, and ensure an integrated approach that satisfies the needs of stakeholders.

To be effective, a review should include a:

- controlled attendance with attendees who will add value;
- defined agenda, including the findings of previous reviews;
- report with clear actions and owners.

Within the UK public sector, a formal process known as 'gateway reviews' is used to ensure that critical projects and programmes are reviewed at appropriate points. This has also been adopted in parts of the private sector.

Project

Product reviews typically provide a quality control mechanism for things that cannot be mechanically or statistically tested. This would, for example, apply to a new process or a software module. In such cases a reviewer would examine or operate them to judge whether they meet the acceptance criteria.

Reviews of the project's business case are usually part of a gate review. They are triggered by the completion of a discrete package of work within the project. There is then a go/no go decision about progressing to the next phase or stage. A review may also be triggered by exceptional circumstances where the project has fallen short of its planned objectives to such a degree that a review is necessary.

A post-project review should be held after the handover of project deliverables, but prior to project closure. Its purpose is to learn lessons and improve the organisation's ability to deliver future projects by:

■ evaluating the effectiveness of project management;
■ comparing what was actually delivered against the original requirements;
■ identifying lessons learned;
■ assessing performance, e.g. comparing the planned schedule against the actual schedule;
■ capturing stakeholders' opinion of how the project was delivered;
■ disseminating findings.

Reviews of the management processes are defined and commissioned by the project sponsor as part of project assurance.

Programme

The programme management team needs to ensure that policies for reviews are implemented consistently across all projects.

As each post-project review is completed, the programme management team also ensures that lessons learned are recorded and made available to subsequent projects.

Quality control reviews are held at programme level as each project hands over its completed output. The programme management team may also be involved in quality reviews of products that form interfaces between projects.

Business case reviews are conducted at the end of each tranche and decisions made whether or not to proceed with the next tranche.

Following a period of business-as-usual operation, a benefits realisation review establishes whether the planned benefits have been fully or partially realised. It identifies any shortfalls and why they occurred. It may be necessary to hold several reviews, depending on when the benefits are expected to be delivered.

3 Delivery

Portfolio

The portfolio life cycle is one of continuous review and relies on information provided by the project and programme reviews.

Project and programme business case reviews collectively indicate the current viability of the portfolio. These are important to identify any project or programme that is unlikely to contribute to portfolio objectives, so that it can be cancelled and its resources released to reshape the portfolio.

There will be formal planned reviews of portfolio performance and these may be aligned to the host organisation's strategic review cycle.

Regular 'assurance' type reviews are scheduled as necessary to maintain the portfolio sponsor's confidence that the component projects and programmes are being well managed.

Further reading

Refer to core texts on pages 4–5.

3.7 **Resource management**

Definition
Resource management comprises the acquisition and deployment of the internal and external resources required to deliver the project, programme or portfolio.

General
The resources needed to deliver a project, programme or portfolio include people, machinery, materials, technology, property and anything else required to deliver the work. Resources may be obtained internally from the host organisation or procured from external sources.

The P3 manager must identify the resources required to deliver the work, as part of planning, and determine when the resources will be required, through scheduling.

The acquisition of external resources will normally be through a procurement process that involves provider selection. This results in a contract for the provision of goods and services. Once a contract is in place, the relationship between the project, programme or portfolio (the buyer) and the provider (the seller) needs to be managed to ensure that the work proceeds according to plan.

Where resources are acquired internally, there may be service-level agreements or terms of reference between the project, programme or portfolio and the department or function providing the resource.

Setting up the management infrastructure is called 'mobilisation'. Projects and programmes are temporary organisations, whereas a portfolio may be permanent or semi-permanent. Therefore, while the infrastructure for managing a portfolio is mobilised once, project and programme infrastructures are mobilised and demobilised on a regular basis.

The policies and procedures to be used for acquiring and deploying resources will be set out in the resource management plan.

Project
Smaller projects will often be completely internal, drawing on the resources of the host organisation. While this means that the project manager may not need considerable expertise in formal procurement and contractual processes, there will be a need for negotiation and influencing skills to compete for the necessary resources. The project sponsor will have a key role to play in ensuring that the host organisation commits to providing the necessary internal resources.

Larger projects will often utilise a mixture of internal and external resources. The project manager may need support from procurement specialists who have expertise in provider selection and contract negotiations.

Programme

The projects and business-as-usual units within a programme will have varying resource needs. The programme manager sets out how the responsibility for managing resources will be shared between project and programme-level management, i.e. implementing an overall strategy while allowing projects to be managed without too much interference.

In preparing the resource management plan, the programme manager will need to consider factors such as:

- How much of the infrastructure can be shared?
- What opportunities are there for pan-programme procurement?
- Are there any projects with very specialised resource requirements?
- Can tranches be structured to make resource usage more efficient?

Resources are an important constraint that will greatly influence how the programme is structured. Programmes have a wide impact on an organisation through the need to implement change and realise benefits, as well as deliver project outputs. All these factors need to be investigated during the definition phase of a programme and the results widely communicated to stakeholders.

Portfolio

The portfolio infrastructure is usually permanent but not necessarily constant. In one strategic planning cycle the portfolio may be very extensive and in another it may be relatively modest. In the course of a planning cycle, the resource demands of a portfolio will vary according to the number of concurrent projects and programmes.

The acquisition and deployment of resources will be an on-going portfolio process in support of the definition and balancing phases of the portfolio life cycle.

Further reading

Association for Project Management, 1998. *Contract strategy for successful project management*. Princes Risborough: Association for Project Management.

Association for Project Management, 1998. *Standard terms for the appointment of a project manager*. Princes Risborough: Association for Project Management.

Broome, J.C., 2002. *Procurement routes for partnering: a practical guide*. London: Thomas Telford.

Office of Government Commerce, 2008. *P30 online repository*.
[online] Available at: www.apm.org.uk/BoK6FurtherReading.

Schwindt, C., 2005. *Resource allocation in project management*. Berlin: Springer.

3.7.1 Contract

Definition

A contract is an agreement made between two or more parties that creates legally binding obligations between them. The contract sets out those obligations and the actions that can be taken if they are not met.

General

Contracts are covered by contract law. Specialist advice should be sought to ensure that the legal ramifications of any proposed contract are fully understood.

The law governing any contract will depend on the applicable jurisdiction. Nevertheless, there are generic principles which are universal in application. There must be:

- an 'offer' made by one party which is 'accepted' unqualified by the other party;
- an intention to create legal relations between the parties and for the parties to be bound by these obligations;
- a consideration passing from one party to the other in return for the provision of goods or services covered by the contract;
- definite terms, so that it is clear as to what conditions the parties are agreeing;
- legality, with only properly incorporated firms or competent persons entering into the contracts.

A contract is required where the resource management plan requires goods or services from outside the host organisation. The resource management plan should set the high-level requirements that the contract needs to implement. For instance, if the plan states that risk should be shared equally between both parties, the contract needs to be appropriately drafted to make sure that this happens.

In many industries a range of standard forms of contract is available. For example, the Joint Contracts Tribunal (JCT) and the New Engineering Contract (NEC) family of contracts provide standard forms of contract that can be utilised in engineering and construction.

The strength of using a standard form of contract is that it will generally take account of established best practice within the particular industry. The weakness is that it may not fully address all the areas within the resource management plan.

Where alterations are made to a standard contract, it then becomes a bespoke contract. A bespoke contract is one that is drafted to suit the specific procurement circumstances. Its strength is that local requirements can be reflected, but this must be traded against the time and cost of producing the document.

The contract itself should contain enough information for the intentions of the parties to be clear. These intentions are set out in the 'contract conditions' and include items such as:

- general information (e.g. who the parties are, description and location of the works or services, legal system that the contract will use, etc.);
- provider's responsibilities for design, approvals, assignment of such responsibilities, subcontracting;
- time: schedule, milestones, completion date;
- quality: testing, defect rectification;
- payment: certificates, release of monies;
- compensation events, change requests, dealing with unforeseen circumstances;
- property: who owns what during the course of the contract, transfer of intellectual property (IP) and copyright;
- assignment and management of risk; the need for insurances;
- how disputes will be managed (e.g. non-performance).

A Statement of Work (SoW) can form a useful annex to the main body of a contract to define the detail of deliverables, timescales and management procedures. It should be noted that such a SoW needs to be drafted to not conflict with the main body and precedence needs to be stated.

The procurement process provides the framework within which all contracts related to the work are managed. In the P3 environment the P3 manager must ensure that the contract is properly executed and placed under version control.

In most circumstances, experienced procurement specialists will be competent to write or check contract documentation, including ensuring that there is a clear hierarchy of conditions and precedence, a clear mechanism for performance management, change management and an exit strategy. This means that the need for advice from lawyers can be restricted to unusual or complex issues.

The P3 manager needs to ensure that the contract is duly executed during the course of the project. This means ensuring that the various legal obligations are discharged by both parties as agreed.

Written contracts can never reflect all possible events. For instance, if a provider is late delivering a particular item of equipment, the P3 manager must decide if the penalties in the contract should be applied. It could be that the provider was waiting for information from another party. Alternatively, the provider may have no legitimate excuse, but the P3 manager may decide not to apply the penalty in order to encourage positive future engagement.

The P3 manager needs to constantly balance the legal environment of the contract with the realities of relationships with providers.

Where multiple contracts exist, the need for coordination is paramount. For instance, if one provider is held up by another provider, is it entitled to an extension of time and does it have a claim against the client organisation? These points should be considered and the contracts drafted accordingly.

Where a provider is allowed to sub-let part of its work, it is generally good practice that the contract between the provider and subcontractor is of a 'back to back' type (i.e. the same philosophy is used in the subcontract as the main contract).

The P3 manager should ensure that the team is aware that contractual obligations can be created inadvertently by poorly worded communications and/or inappropriate actions. Case law has shown that changes to contract have occurred even though no legal instruction was issued. This point should be considered as part of the communication management plan.

At the end of the contract, the P3 manager needs to confirm that all the legal obligations created under the contract have been duly discharged. Items such as equipment warranties and defect liabilities need to be administered for months, if not years, after the contract is concluded. The responsibilities for administering such long-term liabilities need to be considered.

Further reading

Andrews, N., 2011.
Contract law. Cambridge: Cambridge University Press.

Association for Project Management, 1998.
Contract strategy for successful project management. Princes Risborough:
Association for Project Management.

Boundy, C., 2010.
Business contracts handbook. Farnham: Gower.

IACCM, Cummins, T., David, M. and Kawamoto, K., 2011.
Contract and commercial management: the operational guide. Norwich: Van Haren
Publishing.

Longdin, I., 2009.
Legal aspects of purchasing and supply chain management. 3rd ed. Liverpool:
Liverpool Academic.

Turner, R. and Wright, D., 2011.
The commercial management of projects. Burlington, VT: Ashgate.

Ward, G., 2008.
The project manager's guide to purchasing: contracting for goods and services.
Aldershot: Gower.

Wright, D., 2004.
Law for project managers. Aldershot: Gower.

3.7.2 Mobilisation

Definition

Mobilisation ensures that the project, programme or portfolio has appropriate organisational and technical infrastructures and mechanisms for putting resources in place.

General

Initial mobilisation may be performed during the concept and definition phases of a project or programme. This will establish sufficient infrastructure to complete the two initial phases. Full mobilisation will start once approval is given to proceed with the work.

In the portfolio dimension it is simply the decision to operate formal portfolio management that authorises the creation of a suitable infrastructure.

The infrastructure can comprise any of the following:

- the P3 management organisation;
- premises;
- IT and telecoms;
- plant and machinery;
- internal and external resources;
- governance.

The core management organisation is put in place to execute the concept and definition phases of a project or programme. The management organisation is designed during the definition phase and, after approval, the various posts are appointed.

In most cases, the project, programme or portfolio management teams will be located in existing premises. Project management teams should be co-located whenever possible to improve communication and teamwork.

Where it is a large undertaking, or work will be performed by multiple companies in partnership, there will be a case for securing separate premises to provide sufficient space and security of tenure for the duration of the work. Industries such as construction and heavy engineering always need temporary accommodation on site.

The P3 management team may be located within an existing infrastructure, but still have special requirements, e.g. for IT and telecoms. Other examples range from the acquisition of P3 management software to teleconferencing facilities for international, virtual teams.

Because of the temporary nature of projects and programmes, mobilisation will always be followed by demobilisation once the work is complete. This is particularly relevant where capital investment in plant and machinery is needed. Decisions must be made whether to buy, with resale in mind, lease or rent.

The mobilisation of external resources is covered by the provider selection and management process.

Acquiring internal resources often involves a difficult negotiation process. In a matrix organisation, for example, resources may retain their departmental or functional home as well as having a role in a project. The P3 manager may experience conflict with departmental demands when trying to allocate these resources. The decision must then be made whether to rely on informal relationships with departmental managers to gain access to the necessary resources, or whether more formal service-level agreements are needed.

The governance infrastructure covers the establishment of procedures (as laid down in the various management plans) and functions such as P3 assurance and quality assurance.

Project

Projects can range from small internal pieces of work with little or no mobilisation requirement, to major capital projects that may involve acquiring and equipping management premises and production facilities.

The work done to mobilise a major project must be complemented by equal attention to demobilisation. Towards the end of the project, plans must be drawn up to dispose of assets, redeploy staff and possibly reinstate premises to their pre-project condition.

Programme

In mobilising for a programme, the programme management team must consider the needs of the component projects. While the programme management team and its infrastructure will be in place for the duration of the programme, projects will be mobilised and demobilised during the course of the programme life cycle.

The programme management team must consider the impact of the programme schedule on the infrastructure requirements. Some options for the way the tranches of work are structured may have a significant impact on the infrastructure costs. The ability to share the costs of mobilisation across multiple projects must be weighed against the impact on benefits and the business case.

Portfolio

Unlike projects and programmes, the portfolio organisation will have a more permanent basis, although the portfolio may go through multiple planning cycles and be reshaped according to the needs of the latest strategic plan. Therefore, portfolio mobilisation is a one-off project that sets up the infrastructure required to coordinate projects and programmes through multiple strategic cycles.

A committed and robust portfolio infrastructure forms the basis for an organisation to become increasingly mature in its ability to deliver projects and programmes. It may be set up to include permanent organisational structures as, for example, the creation of an enterprise project management office to provide support at all levels. There may also be communities of practice to support the continual improvement of individual competence, or professional development programmes to encourage professionalism.

The mobilisation of a portfolio requires board-level support to ensure that it is done thoroughly from the start. Only then will the portfolio infrastructure be embedded in the organisation as the preferred way of delivering projects and programmes.

Further Reading

Costin, A.A., 2008.
Managing difficult projects. Amsterdam: Butterworth Heinemann.

3.7.3 Procurement

Definition
Procurement is the process by which products and services are acquired from an external provider for incorporation into the project, programme or portfolio.

General
In procurement, an external source represents anything outside the project, programme or portfolio. External sources will often be supplier or contractor organisations, but may also be another department or division of the host organisation.

Where the external source is a separate legal entity, the terms under which goods and services are procured will be the subject of a legal contract. When the source is part of the same organisation, a service-level agreement may be used.

Procurement typically covers the acquisition of:

- standard 'off the shelf' goods and services;
- goods or services that are designed and provided specifically for the purchaser;
- professional advice or consultancy.

The work involved in procuring resources can be a significant project in itself. The way procurement is to be managed is set out in the resource management plan. This describes how to acquire and manage the goods and services required. The plan covers factors such as the:

- 'make' or 'buy' decision;
- use of single, integrated or multiple providers;
- required provider relationships;
- provider selection;
- conditions and forms of contract;
- types of pricing and methods of reimbursement.

In some projects, programmes or portfolios, procured resources can represent the majority of the cost, so a rigorous procurement process is vital to success. All procurement involves risk and all aspects of the resource management plan must be prepared with risk management in mind.

One example is the choice of payment methods, which include:

- fixed price (low risk to the buyer but needs a detailed specification);
- cost plus fee (used where scope is flexible but has greater risk of cost overrun);
- per unit quantity (for use where units are well defined but numbers are indeterminate);
- target cost (where risk is shared and the provider is rewarded for cost savings).

A package breakdown structure, based on a product or work breakdown structure, shows how the scope of work will be arranged in order to procure packages from different providers. The allocation of work to these packages is another important mechanism for managing risk.

For each package, the relative emphasis on time, cost, quality, and the tolerances on each, needs to be considered. For instance, if a package is on the critical path of the project, then there will be greater emphasis on time performance. Consciously addressing these factors greatly influences how contract incentives are designed.

Ethical procurement is also important. A P3 management team needs to be able to demonstrate that its procurement practices are ethical and transparent, and that good governance, corporate accountability and probity are being observed.

Project

Stand-alone projects may be able to take advantage of procurement arrangements set up by the host organisation. Similarly, those that are part of a programme or portfolio may find that much of the procurement is handled at the higher level.

When a project has specialist, or unique, requirements it will need access to procurement specialists and must consider procurement implications as early in the life cycle as is practicable. Waiting until the full approval of the project at the end of the definition phase may, for example, result in tender delays and long lead times having a detrimental effect on the schedule.

Programme

The size of a programme may enable economies of scale through consolidating and coordinating the procurement needs of multiple projects. An overall resource management plan for the programme will govern how projects acquire goods and services.

A programme may be able to make use of partnering and alliancing to create long-term relationships with providers. It may also be able to set up enabling contracts that agree unit prices for goods and services that can be called off by individual projects.

Portfolio

A portfolio, and all its component projects and programmes, should take advantage of organisational-level procurement resources. If such facilities do not exist, the scale of a portfolio may justify investment in e-procurement, for example, or creating lists of preferred providers.

Stakeholder management of providers, through conferences and regular communication to foster a partnership approach, can be justified at the portfolio level for the benefit of component projects and programmes.

Further reading

Broome, J.C., 2002.
Procurement routes for partnering: a practical guide. London: Thomas Telford.

Department for Enterprise, Trade and Employment, 2009.
The 10 step guide to SMART procurement and SME access to public contracts.
[online] Available at: www.apm.org.uk/BoK6FurtherReading.

3.7.4 Provider selection and management

Definition

Provider selection and management is the process of identifying, selecting, appointing and supervising providers through the P3 life cycle.

General

Provider management continues throughout the life cycle. The process will vary in detail from one sector to another but generally follows six steps. It needs to be scaled to be fit for purpose and should be neither onerous nor superficial. The process should be reviewed and approved by appropriate stakeholders and documented in the resource management plan.

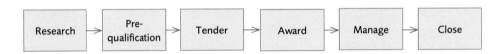

Figure 3.13: Provider selection and management process

The research step involves identifying the providers that have the required capability. This may be unnecessary where there is already a regularly reviewed and up-to-date approved provider list.

Research may result in a long list of potential providers. Pre-qualification seeks to reduce this list by a number of means. A typical approach is to send out a pre-qualification questionnaire to gather information from potential providers. This may clarify the production capacity of the provider, their willingness to tender, their financial stability and their technical experience. It may also ask for references for similar work.

The pre-qualification results in a shortlist of providers who will be asked to provide a full bid against a defined set of requirements. Tendering is an important process in its own right and a P3 manager may need to seek specialist help. It is important that the requirements are clear and all providers are given an equal chance of success.

Records associated with selection should be maintained and archived to contain risks associated with potential challenges by unsuccessful providers. Inputs to the selection process should include an appropriate risk analysis in addition to cost, time and quality considerations as defined in the resource management plan. Where possible, a reserve provider should be identified. For critical goods and services the contract may be split amongst several providers as a form of risk containment.

Award will involve the negotiation and agreement of a contract to supply goods and services. Attention needs to be paid throughout the whole selection process to ensure that a contract is not casually entered into, and it should be made clear in all meetings and in associated documents that the proceedings are subject to contract.

Once a contract is awarded, it is important that the relationship between the project, programme or portfolio and the provider is actively managed. Although much effort may have been invested in the binding contract, resorting to the contract to resolve disputes should be seen as a last resort. P3 managers must regard providers as members of the team and communicate effectively.

Once the goods or services to be supplied by the provider have been delivered and accepted, the contract will be closed. This will involve ensuring that all financial arrangements have been honoured, all changes to the contract have been accounted for, and may involve setting up a maintenance contract to support, repair or upgrade goods provided.

Project

The shorter timescale of projects means that provider selection may be focused entirely on the optimisation of cost, timescale and quality of delivery of the specific requirement. Scaling of the selection process will be of high importance, as selection costs will need to be funded entirely from the project budget.

A project manager wishing to procure a solution to complex or innovative requirements may not know exactly how best to meet the requirements and may enter into a dialogue with potential providers to help develop a solution. Where this is the case, clear rules on disclosure of information from one potential provider to another need to be established and maintained, both for the reputation of the purchaser and for legal compliance.

On smaller projects there will be less opportunity for the project manager to develop a relationship with the provider. In such situations the selection process needs to ensure that the mechanisms for supplying the goods or services are as routine and low risk as possible.

Programme

The programme management team will decide whether providers are to be handled at project or programme level. Typical situations to consider are:

- providers supplying goods or services to multiple projects;
- specialist providers working on one project;
- risky contracts that need specialist procurement expertise;
- routine supplies;
- on-going maintenance that supports benefits realisation.

All these factors will be taken into account when preparing the resource management plan.

Portfolio

Portfolio management teams have the greatest opportunity to consider long-term partnerships with providers. A portfolio can set up 'framework agreements' with providers. The portfolio management team will complete the selection process and set up contracts that projects and programmes can use to call off goods or services at agreed rates. This greatly reduces the effort required for the selection process.

The relationship with framework providers will be handled at portfolio level but there will still be many providers that have to be selected to meet the demands of individual projects and programmes. The portfolio management team will set out the process to be used and will maintain an overview to identify common needs.

Further reading

Beil, D., 2009.
Supplier selection.
[online] Available at: www.apm.org.uk/BoK6FurtherReading.

Chartered Institute of Purchasing & Supply, 2007.
Developing and implementing a strategic sourcing strategy.
[online] Available at: www.apm.org.uk/BoK6FurtherReading.

Chartered Institute of Purchasing & Supply, 2007.
Supply chain management.
[online] Available at: www.apm.org.uk/BoK6FurtherReading.

Lewis, H., 2005.
Bids, tenders and proposals: winning business through best practice. 2nd ed.
London: Kogan Page.

National Health Service, 2010.
Procurement guide for commissioners of NHS-funded services.
[online] Available at: www.apm.org.uk/BoK6FurtherReading.

Nickson, D., 2008.
The bid manager's handbook. Aldershot: Gower.

Office of Government Commerce, 2009.
Requirement to distinguish between "selection" and "award" stages of a public procurement, and to give suppliers complete information about the criteria used in both stages – Action Note.
[online] Available at: www.apm.org.uk/BoK6FurtherReading.

Sant, T., 2004.
Persuasive business proposals: writing to win more customers, clients and contracts. 2nd ed. New York, NY: Amacom.

4 Interfaces

There are many areas where P3 management interfaces with other disciplines. Project, programme and portfolio managers need to have an understanding of how disciplines such as law, accounting and HR management impact upon their work.

They do not have to become experts in these disciplines, but they do need to understand them sufficiently in order to look for expert help and to ask the right questions.

The need to understand these disciplines increases with the progression from project to portfolio-level management. Managers of smaller projects will rely on specialist support from within their organisation, whereas managers of portfolios will often need a good understanding of these topics at a strategic level.

4.1 **Accounting**

Definition

Accounting is the process of collecting and communicating financial information to meet legal requirements, business management requirements, plus internal and external stakeholders' needs.

General

Different forms of accounting are used in an organisation to provide information for statutory purposes and for running the business.

Financial accounting follows strict procedures to monitor the business and provides accounts that meet the needs of the tax authorities, shareholders, internal and external stakeholders, and the board. Management accounts are much more flexible in content and provide information that is essential for the business to function and for managers to make day-to-day decisions.

P3 managers need to understand at least the basics of financial accounting terms and techniques. However, the world of the P3 manager is dominated by the need to track and control finance. So, a detailed understanding of the accounting needs of projects, programmes and portfolios, plus an understanding of the relationship with the organisation's financial accounting systems and reporting, is essential.

It is useful for P3 managers to be able to interpret and evaluate a balance sheet and profit and loss statements. This enables them to understand, for example, the finances of the host organisation, partners or providers. Particularly at programme and portfolio level, P3 managers will need to communicate with sponsors and finance directors where a mutual understanding of financial terms is essential.

Financial accounting is not designed to provide information specifically for the needs of P3 management. These are met by tools and reports that track expenditure in real time and produce forecasts that allow decisions to be made. Reports from P3 accounting are aggregated at programme and portfolio level to enable strategic decisions.

Financial information from an organisation's range of projects, programmes and portfolios needs to be monitored and tracked. In many organisations this is achieved through links between P3 IT systems and the financial accounting IT systems.

Further reading

Refer to core texts on pages 4–5.

4.2 **Health and safety**

Definition
Health and safety management is the process of identifying and minimising threats to workers and those affected by the work throughout the project, programme and portfolio life cycle.

General
The P3 management team needs to consider health and safety across the entire life cycle, starting at the concept phase and continuing through to closure. This involves:

- establishing a health and safety policy and its systematic implementation;
- utilising proactive and reactive performance measures to gain assurance of compliance;
- measuring effectiveness in driving good health and safety performance (these measures can include audits, inspections and a review of safety performance data).

All managers are responsible for ensuring that the work under their control complies with all relevant health and safety legislation. They play a critical role in leading by example and ensuring that the team develops a good health and safety culture.

They need to have a good overview of the applicable legislation but are not expected to be experts in health and safety. They are required to seek competent advice to assist them in discharging their responsibilities.

As well as legal duties, there is also a moral obligation to protect people from harm. P3 managers' duties are twofold. Firstly, they have a duty to ensure the health and safety of the team. Secondly, they must ensure that the work is delivered in a way that manages relevant risks throughout the life cycle.

Many industries and sectors are highly regulated. These will require the P3 manager to have an understanding of the specific regulatory framework, for example, in nuclear, railways, and construction. Managers must also be aware of any applicable product safety legislation, particularly where a product is being developed in one country for use in another.

The two key pieces of UK legislation are the Health and Safety at Work Act 1974, and the Management of Health and Safety at Work Regulations 1999.

The basic requirements of the Health and Safety at Work Act are for employers to secure the health, safety and welfare of employees and to ensure that others who may be affected by the works are protected (this may include contractors, visitors, members of the public, delivery personnel, etc.).

The Management of Health and Safety at Work Regulations require risk assessments to be undertaken and for competent advice to be sought.

Similar legislation may be found throughout the world and P3 managers must always ensure compliance with the relevant legislation of the country in which the work is being undertaken.

P3 managers need to identify health and safety risks and plan for their elimination or reduction to an acceptable level ('As Low as Reasonably Practicable – ALARP'). These risks can be recorded and managed alongside other project risks.

Assurance is a key aspect of P3 management and the P3 sponsor must gain assurance that all health and safety requirements are being met throughout the life cycle.

Further reading

HM Government.
Health and safety at work. Available at: www.apm.org.uk/BoK6FurtherReading.

4.3 **Human resource management**

Definition
Human resource management (HRM) is about managing people-related activities within an organisation to meet its strategic goals.

General
HRM is concerned with every aspect of the use and development of people within an organisation, whether related to business-as-usual or project and programme activities.

It has a wide scope, encompassing such areas as recruitment, competency development, legislation, disputes, personal development, and rewards and incentives.

P3 managers work closely with HRM both to secure resources and monitor their progress, as well as ensuring that skills and training needs are met for their teams. So, they need an understanding, not only of the specific HR requirements within their work areas, but also a wide general understanding of the implications of HRM within the organisation.

Apart from legislative requirements, the application of HRM policy will depend on the structure and culture of the organisation. HRM in a project-based organisation is likely to be closely aligned to the needs of P3 managers, for example, in keeping a database of the availability of resources with specialist skills. In other organisations there may be less awareness of specific P3 resourcing requirements.

In a matrix environment the P3 manager often has responsibility but little power. Team members will report to a line manager who is responsible, together with HRM, for their performance appraisal, promotion and pay reviews. This requires diplomacy and leadership skills from the P3 manager and an understanding by HRM of the balance needed between projects, programmes and business-as-usual.

HRM specialists in the organisation may be available to the P3 manager. Their knowledge of employee relations, resourcing, organisation and legal factors can contribute to project, programme and portfolio success.

Best practice in HRM establishes an environment in which an organisation can flourish. It helps prevent disputes and disruption, and encourages such policies as diversity and equality.

Recruitment, induction and training, forecasting resources and performance management are among the areas that require close collaboration between P3 managers and HRM.

Dealing with the transient nature of the P3 environment and the likelihood of working arrangements relying on remote or disparate teams, brings challenges beyond those experienced in operational management. Effective communication between HR and P3 managers is essential to help solve any conflict and achieve effective management.

HRM will be involved, together with P3 managers, in knowledge management and establishing competence frameworks that help develop the P3 maturity of the organisation. As projects and programmes come and go, HRM can also become a repository of experience about the HR needs of projects. For programmes and portfolios it can be the means of providing continuity as the mix of personnel changes over a long period.

Further reading

Chartered Institute of Personnel and Development, 2011.
Strategic human resource management.
[online] Available at: www.apm.org.uk/BoK6FurtherReading.

4.4 Law

Definition

The relevant legal duties, rights and processes that should be applied to projects, programmes and portfolios.

General

P3 managers must operate within the law and have an awareness of the legal systems in the jurisdictions in which they operate. Obvious areas of the law that P3 managers must take into account include:

- health and safety legislation;
- employment legislation;
- contract legislation.

In different industry sectors a much wider knowledge may be needed, including environmental or intellectual property law, or the regulatory environment in nuclear or rail work.

In the UK there are essentially two types of law – criminal and civil. In general, P3 managers' primary concerns will be with the civil law, but some breaches of civil law may constitute a criminal offence. For example, a gross breach of Health and Safety legislation where death of an employee results may give rise to prosecution for the criminal offence of manslaughter.

Civil law is primarily governed by statute, but this is interpreted by the judiciary, so that legal precedents are established through case law. Statute law in the UK is contained in primary legislation enacted by Parliament, and in secondary legislation (statutory instruments).

Most UK legislation is subject to the overriding authority of the European Parliament and the European Convention of Human Rights (ECHR). This affects many areas of relevance to P3 managers, for example, the Working Time Directive or the consolidated directive on public procurement.

Failure to comply with the civil law may result in punitive fines and compensation for any injured parties.

UK law governs England and Wales, and Northern Ireland law governs Northern Ireland. Scotland has its own jurisdiction, legislation and terminology. Although there is wide overlap, there are some fundamental differences particularly in relation to property and contract law.

It is fairly obvious that a project or programme being undertaken in a particular country will be subject to the legal jurisdiction of that country. But in a world of outsourced projects, joint ventures, and virtual teams, the legal environment can be extremely complex and jurisdiction may not be as obvious as it seems. In all these circumstances the P3 manager must have sufficient knowledge to call on, and act on, expert advice.

Further reading

Refer to core texts on pages 4–5.

4.5 **Security**

Definition

Security within projects, programmes and portfolios concerns the identification, assessment and mitigation of the risks posed to information, assets and people.

General

Organisations have a legal and a moral duty to protect their information, assets and people. In the P3 environment this is the responsibility of the P3 manager and the sponsor.

Security is a vital component in building trust with customers and partners whether they be businesses or individuals. It can also be a legal requirement, as in the need to secure confidential data.

It involves many different issues and solutions and requires a systems thinking approach taking into account people, process, technology and governance. Failure to operate in a holistic mode means that security vulnerabilities may be left open to exploitation.

The risks of loss and compromise must be assessed at all key stages of the work, either in the normal course of delivery or when significant change occurs.

Like quality, addressing security at the earliest stages of a project or programme is critical to ensuring that mitigation measures can be developed in as cost effective way as possible and with minimum disruption. In many cases, simple measures taken early can remove the requirement for much more costly and awkward measures later on. Security must be embedded at the concept and definition phases of the life cycle.

The P3 manager and sponsor must:

- ensure that security goals are identified, meet stakeholder requirements and are integrated with relevant processes;
- formulate, review and approve the security policy;
- review the effectiveness of the security policy;
- provide clear direction and visible management support for security initiatives;
- provide the resources needed for security;
- approve the assignment of specific roles and responsibilities for security across the P3 organisation;
- initiate plans to maintain security awareness.

The approach to security should align with processes such as risk management, health and safety and organisational policy. The required level of security must be achieved without compromising delivery.

Further reading

Cabinet Office, 2009.
Cyber security strategy of the United Kingdom: safety, security and resilience in cyber space. Norwich: The Stationery Office.

Cabinet Office, 2011.
HMG security policy framework.
[online] Available at: www.apm.org.uk/BoK6FurtherReading.

HM Government, 1998.
Data protection act. Available at: www.apm.org.uk/BoK6FurtherReading.

HM Government, 2010.
UK national security strategy. Available at: www.apm.org.uk/BoK6FurtherReading.

HM Government, 1998. Data protection act. [online] Available at: www.apm.org.uk/BoK6FurtherReading.

International Organisation for Standardisation, 2010-11.
ISO/IEC 27001 to 27006 (information security).
Available at: www.apm.org.uk/BoK6FurtherReading.

4.6 **Sustainability**

Definition

Sustainability describes an environmental, social and economically integrated approach to development that meets present needs without compromising the environment for future generations.

General

The term sustainable development was defined by the Brundtland Commission in the 1980s and is a simple concept that can often be difficult to put into practice. In P3 management, it involves both individual and corporate responsibility to ensure that outputs, outcomes and benefits are not only sustainable over their life cycles, but are sustainable during their creation.

The ability of P3 managers to influence the sustainability of their work may be constrained by the host or client organisation.

The three strands that need to be considered in any sustainability assessment relate to the environmental, economic and social dimensions of any work.

These strands are clearer in some sectors than others. Large-scale engineering and construction projects will often have an immediate impact on the environment. These will be closely monitored and often be subject to legislative environmental requirements. However, work involving organisational change or the production of software, may not immediately register as having an environmental impact.

The need for sustainable development stems from the recognition that using natural and human resources indiscriminately to achieve growth and 'single bottom line' financial profit, without regard to the environmental or social cost, is no longer tenable.

Many organisations now recognise that the environmental and social, as well as the economic, dimensions of business activity need to be factored into their management strategies. This is sometimes referred to as the 'triple bottom line'.

All members of the P3 team can have an influence, however small, on sustainability and should think creatively about how they can act responsibly in their day-to-day work. For example, this may well be something as simple as reducing unnecessary travel, or the use of paper. Increased seniority gives P3 managers wider influence. They can create an environment where sustainability is a factor in planning and implementing work. They will have influence with clients and sponsors and, from the concept phase, can challenge aspects of sustainability.

Sustainability should be considered in many different core areas of project, programme and portfolio management. For example, in procurement there will be opportunities to buy from sustainable sources and to make the supply chain more efficient. Risk management will consider the threats and opportunities stemming from innovative but sustainable approaches, and consider the environmental risks of proposed solutions.

At programme and portfolio level, P3 managers need to play a part in analysing and selecting projects to meet sustainability objectives wherever possible. Within a portfolio, P3 managers need to liaise with the sponsors and organisational boards to explain how they support the sustainable objectives of the organisation.

Sustainable development is an area in continual flux and is rarely without debate and argument. There are often no hard and fast rules unless the work is in a highly regulated environment. However, any manager needs to consider it as a core aspect of being a professional and ethical manager.

Further reading

Edwards, B., 2005.
Rough guide to sustainability. London: RIBA Enterprises.

Gro Harlem Bruntland (Bruntland Commission), 1987.
Our common future. Oxford: Oxford University Press.

Taylor, T., 2011.
Sustainability interventions – for managers of projects and programmes.
London: Dashdot Publications.

Glossary

This glossary is made up of terms used in the sixth edition of the *APM Body of Knowledge* only. Definitions are provided where terms used are unique to the profession, or have a unique meaning in the profession.

Accept A response to a threat where no course of action is taken.

Acceptance criteria The requirements and essential conditions that have to be achieved before a deliverable is accepted.

Accounting The process of collecting and communicating financial information to meet legal requirements, business management requirements, plus internal and external stakeholders' needs.

Activity 1. A task, job, operation or process consuming time and possibly other resources.

2. The smallest self-contained unit of work in a project.

Activity duration The length of time that it takes to complete an activity.

Activity-on-node network A network diagram where the activities are represented by the nodes.

Actual expenditure The costs that have been charged to the budget and for which payment has been made, or accrued.

Actual progress A measure of the work that has been completed for comparison with the baseline.

Agile A family of development methodologies where requirements and solutions are developed iteratively and incrementally throughout the life cycle.

Analogous estimating See comparative estimating.

Analytical estimating See bottom-up estimating.

Avoid A response to a threat that eliminates its probability or impact on the project.

Balance A phase in the portfolio life cycle where the component projects and programmes are balanced in terms of risk, resource usage, cash flow and impact across the business.

Baseline The reference levels against which a project, programme or portfolio is monitored and controlled.

Benefit The quantifiable and measurable improvement resulting from completion of deliverables that is perceived as positive by a stakeholder. It will normally have a tangible value, expressed in monetary terms that will justify the investment.

Benefits management The identification, definition, planning, tracking and realisation of business benefits.

Benefits realisation The practice of ensuring that benefits are derived from outputs and outcomes.

Blueprint A document defining and describing what a programme is designed to achieve in terms of the business and operational vision.

Board A body that provides sponsorship to a project, programme or portfolio. The board will represent financial, provider and user interests.

Bottom-up estimating An estimating technique that uses detailed specifications to estimate time and cost for each product or activity.

Breakdown structure A hierarchical structure by which project elements are broken down, or decomposed. Examples include: cost breakdown structure (CBS), organisational breakdown structure (OBS), product breakdown structure (PBS), and work breakdown structure (WBS).

Brief The output of the concept phase of a project or programme.

Budgeting and cost control The estimation of costs, the setting of an agreed budget, and management of actual and forecast costs against that budget.

Buffer A term used in critical chain for the centralised management of contingencies.

Business-as-usual An organisation's normal day-to-day operations.

Business case Provides justification for undertaking a project or programme. It evaluates the benefit, cost and risk of alternative options and provides a rationale for the preferred solution.

Business change manager The role responsible for benefits management from identification through to realisation.

Business risk assessment The assessment of risk to business objectives rather than risk to achieving project, programme or portfolio objectives.

Categorise A phase in the portfolio life cycle where the component projects and programmes may be grouped according to shared characteristics.

Change control The process through which all requests to change the baseline scope of a project, programme or portfolio are captured, evaluated and then approved, rejected or deferred.

Change freeze A point after which no further changes to scope will be considered.

Change management Change management is a structured approach to moving an organisation from the current state to the desired future state.

Change register A record of all proposed changes to scope.

Change request A request to obtain formal approval for changes to the scope of work.

Closure The formal end point of a project or programme, either because it has been completed or because it has been terminated early.

Collaborative negotiation Negotiation that seeks to create a 'win-win' scenario where all parties involved get part or all of what they were looking for from the negotiation.

Committed expenditure Costs that have not yet been paid but cannot be cancelled.

Communication The means by which information or instructions are exchanged.

Successful communication occurs when the received meaning is the same as the transmitted meaning.

Communities of practice Groups of people who share a concern or passion for an aspect of P3 management and develop expertise through regular interaction.

Comparative estimating An estimating technique based on the comparison with, and factoring from, the cost of similar, previous work.

Competence The combined knowledge, skill and behaviour that a person needs to perform properly in a job or work role.

Competence framework A set of competences and competencies that may be used to define a role.

Competency A personal attribute of an individual.

Complexity Complexity relates to the degree of interaction of all the elements that comprise P3 management and is dependent on such factors as the level of risk, range of stakeholders and degree of innovation.

Concept Concept is the first phase in the project or programme life cycle. During this phase the need, opportunity or problem is confirmed, the overall

feasibility of the work is considered and a preferred solution identified.

Configuration Functional and physical characteristics of a product as defined in its specification.

Configuration management Configuration management encompasses the administrative activities concerned with the creation, maintenance, controlled change and quality control of the scope of work.

Conflict management The process of identifying and addressing differences that, if left unresolved, could affect objectives.

Consumable resource A type or resource that only remains available until consumed (for example a material).

Context A collective term for the governance and setting of a project, programme or portfolio.

Contingency Resource set aside for responding to identified risks.

Contract An agreement made between two or more parties that creates legally binding obligations between them. The contract sets out those obligations and the actions that can be taken if they are not met.

Control Tracking performance against agreed plans and taking the corrective action required to meet defined objectives.

Criticality Used in Monte Carlo analysis, the criticality index represents the percentage of calculations that resulted in the activity being placed on the critical path.

Critical chain A networking technique that identifies paths through a project based on resource dependencies, as well as technical dependencies.

Critical path A sequence of activities through a network diagram from start to finish, the sum of whose durations determines the overall duration. There may be more than one such path.

Critical path analysis The procedure for calculating the critical path and floats in a network diagram.

Cybernetic control The form of control that deals with routine progress tracking and corrective action using a feedback loop.

Define The phase of a portfolio life cycle where the projects, programmes and change to business-as-usual required to meet strategic objectives are identified and evaluated.

Defined The third level of a typical maturity model where processes are documented and standardised.

Definition The second phase of a project or programme life cycle where requirements are refined, the preferred solution is identified and ways of achieving it are identified.

Delegation The practice of giving a person or group the authority to perform the responsibilities of, or act on behalf of, another.

Deliverable A product, set of products or package of work that will be delivered to, and formally accepted by, a stakeholder.

Demobilisation The controlled dispersal of personnel and disposal of assets when they are no longer needed on a project, programme or portfolio.

Dependency A relationship between activities in a network diagram.

Disbenefit A consequence of change perceived as negative by one or more stakeholders.

Do nothing option The result or consequence of not proceeding with the project or programme. Usually explained in the business case.

Drawdown The removal of funds from an agreed source resulting in a reduction of available funds.

Earned value The value of completed work expressed in terms of the budget assigned to that work. A measure of progress which may be expressed in cost or labour hours.

Earned value management A project control process, based on a structured approach to planning, cost collection and performance measurement. It facilitates the integration of project scope, time and cost objectives and the establishment of a baseline plan of performance measurement.

Enhance A response to an opportunity that increases its probability, impact or both.

Enterprise project management office An organisation that is responsible for the governance infrastructure of P3 management.

Environment The circumstances and conditions within which the project, programme or portfolio must operate.

Escalation The process by which issues are drawn to the attention of a higher level of management.

Estimate An approximation of time and cost targets, refined throughout the life cycle.

Estimating The use of a range of tools and techniques to produce estimates.

Estimating funnel A representation of the increasing levels of estimating accuracy that can be achieved through the phases of the life cycle.

Ethics frameworks Sets recognised standards of conduct and behaviour within the P3 profession.

Event-driven Control actions or reports that are triggered by a specific event are referred to as 'event-driven'.

Exploit A response to an opportunity that maximises both its probability and impact.

Extended life cycle A life cycle model that includes the operation of outputs and realisation of benefits.

Financial management The process of estimating and justifying costs in order to secure funds, controlling expenditure and evaluating the outcomes.

Finish-to-finish A dependency in an activity-on-node network. It indicates that one activity cannot finish until another activity has finished.

Finish-to-start A dependency in an activity-on-node network. It indicates that one activity cannot start until another activity has finished.

Float A term used to describe the flexibility with which an activity may be rescheduled. There are various types of float, such as total float and free float.

Forecast expenditure The estimated and predicted use of money.

Funding The means by which the capital required to undertake a project, programme or portfolio is secured and then made available as required.

Gantt chart A graphical representation of activity against time. Variations may include information such as 'actual vs. planned', resource usage and dependencies.

Gate The point between phases, gates and/or tranches where a go/no go decision can be made about the remainder of the work.

Go/No go A form of control where a decision is made whether or not to continue with the work.

Governance The set of policies, regulations, functions, processes, procedures and responsibilities that define the establishment, management and control of projects, programmes or portfolios.

Handover The point in the life cycle where deliverables are handed over to the sponsor and users.

Health and safety management
The process of identifying and minimising threats to workers and those affected by the work throughout the project, programme or portfolio life cycle.

Host organisation The organisation that provides the strategic direction of the project, programme or portfolio and will be the primary recipient of the benefits.

Human resource management (HRM) Managing people-related activities within an organisation to meet its strategic goals.

Influencing The act of affecting the behaviours and actions of others.

Information management The collection, storage, dissemination, archiving and destruction of information. It enables teams and stakeholders to use their time, resource and expertise effectively to make decisions and to fulfil their roles.

Infrastructure Provides support for projects, programmes and portfolios, and is the focal point for the development and maintenance of P3 management within an organisation.

Initial The first level of a typical maturity model where processes are typically ad hoc and occasionally chaotic.

Integrated assurance The coordination of assurance activities where there are a number of assurance providers.

Integrative management The application of management processes that integrate some or all fundamental components of scope, schedule, cost, risk, quality and resources.

Interpersonal skills The means by which people relate to, and interact with, other people.

Investment appraisal A collection of techniques used to identify the attractiveness of an investment.

Issue A formal issue occurs when the tolerances of delegated work are predicted to be exceeded or have been exceeded. This triggers the escalation of the issue from one level of management to the next in order to seek a solution.

Knowledge management The systematic management of information and learning. It turns personal information and experience into collective knowledge that can be widely shared throughout an organisation and a profession.

Law The relevant legal duties, rights and processes that should be applied to projects, programmes and portfolios.

Leadership The ability to establish vision and direction, to influence and align others towards a common purpose, and to empower and inspire people to achieve success.

Learning and development The continual improvement of competence at all levels of an organisation.

Lessons learned Documented experiences that can be used to improve the future management of projects, programmes and portfolios.

APM Body of Knowledge 6th edition

Life cycle The inter-related phases of a project, programme or portfolio and provides a structure for governing the progression of work.

Linear sequential model See waterfall method.

Line-of-balance A scheduling technique for delivery of repetitive products that shows how resource teams move from product to product rather than the detail of individual activities.

Managed The fourth level of a typical capability maturity model where metrics are gathered on process performance and used to control future performance.

Management plan A plan that sets out the policies and principles that will be applied to the management of some aspects of a project, programme or portfolio. Examples include a Risk Management Plan, a Communication Management Plan and a Quality Management Plan.

Management reserve A sum of money held as an overall contingency to cover the cost impact of some unexpected event.

Maturity model An organisational model that describes a number of evolutionary stages through which an organisation improves its management processes.

Milestone A key event selected for its importance in the schedule.

Mobilisation Ensures that the project, programme or portfolio has appropriate organisational and technical infrastructures and mechanisms for putting resources in place.

Monte Carlo analysis A technique used to estimate the likely range of outcomes from a complex process by simulating the process under randomly selected conditions a large number of times.

Negotiation A discussion between two or more parties aimed at reaching agreement.

Network analysis A collective term for the different ways in which a network diagram may be analysed including, for example, critical path analysis, program evaluation and review technique, and critical chain.

Network diagram A model of activities and their dependencies comprising nodes and links.

Objectives Predetermined results towards which effort is directed. Objectives may be defined in terms of outputs, outcomes and/or benefits.

Operations management The management of those activities that create the core services or products provided by an organisation.

Opportunity A positive risk event that, if it occurs, will have a beneficial effect on achievement of objectives.

Optimising The fifth and last level of a typical maturity model where continuous process improvement is enabled by quantitative feedback from the process and from piloting innovative ideas and technologies.

Organisation The management structure applicable to the project, programme or portfolio and the organisational environment in which it operates.

Outcome The changed circumstances or behaviour that results from the use of an output.

Output The tangible or intangible product typically delivered by a project.

P3 assurance The process of providing confidence to stakeholders that projects, programmes and portfolios will achieve their scope, time, cost and quality objectives, and realise their benefits.

P3 management The collective term for project, programme and portfolio management.

P3 management team A collective term for those involved in the sponsorship and day-to-day management of a project, programme or portfolio.

Parallel life cycle A life cycle where phases are conducted in parallel.

Parametric estimating An estimating technique that uses a statistical relationship between historic data and other variables to calculate an estimate.

Phase The major subdivision of a life cycle.

Planning Determines what is to be delivered, how much it will cost, when it will be delivered, how it will be delivered and who will carry it out.

Portfolio A grouping of an organisation's projects and programmes. Portfolios can be managed at an organisational or functional level.

Portfolio management The selection, prioritisation and control of an organisation's projects and programmes in line with its strategic objectives and capacity to deliver.

Precedence network A network diagram in which activities are represented by rectangles (nodes) and their dependencies are represented by arrows.

PRINCE2™ A project management methodology. It is an acronym standing for PRojects IN Controlled Environments.

Prioritise The phase of a portfolio life cycle where priorities are set by strategic objective, return on investment or any other chosen metric.

Procurement Procurement is the process by which products and services are acquired from an external provider for incorporation into the project, programme or portfolio.

Product A tangible or intangible component of a project's output. Synonymous with deliverable.

Professionalism The application of expert and specialised knowledge within a specific field and the acceptance of standards relating to that profession.

Program evaluation and review technique A network analysis technique that calculates standard deviations for the schedule based on three-point estimates of activity durations.

Programme A group of related projects and change management activities that together achieve beneficial change for an organisation.

Programme management The coordinated management of projects and change management activities to achieve beneficial change.

Project A unique, transient endeavour undertaken to achieve planned objectives.

Project management The application of processes, methods, knowledge, skills and experience to achieve the project objectives.

Project management plan (PMP) The output of the definition phase of a project or programme.

Provider A person or company that provides goods or services.

Provider selection and management The processes of identifying and selecting management providers through the P3 life cycle.

Quality The fitness for purpose or the degree of conformance of the outputs of a process or the process itself.

Quality management A discipline for ensuring the outputs, benefits and the processes by which they are delivered, meet stakeholder requirements and are fit for purpose.

Reduce A response to a threat that reduces its probability, impact or both.

Reject A response to an opportunity where no action is taken.

Repeatable The second level of a typical maturity model where basic processes are established and the necessary discipline is in place to repeat earlier successes.

Reports 1. The presentation of information in an appropriate format (e.g. management report).

2. A written record or summary, a detailed account or statement, or a verbal account.

Requirements management The process of capturing, assessing and justifying stakeholders' wants and needs.

Resource allocation The process by which resources are attributed to activities.

Resource availability The level of availability of a resource, which may vary over time.

Resource levelling A scheduling calculation that delays activities such that resource usage is kept below specified limits. It is also known as resource limited scheduling.

Resource management The acquisition and deployment of the internal and external resources required to deliver the project, programme or portfolio.

Resources All those items required to undertake work including people, finance and materials.

Resource scheduling A collection of techniques used to calculate the resources required to deliver the work and when they will be required.

Resource smoothing A scheduling calculation that involves utilising float or increasing or decreasing the resources required for specific activities, such that any peaks and troughs of resource usage are smoothed out. This does not affect the overall duration. It is also known as time limited resource scheduling.

Responsibility assignment matrix A diagram or chart showing assigned responsibilities for elements of work. It is created by combining the work breakdown structure with the organisational breakdown structure.

Re-usable resource A resource that when no longer needed becomes available for other uses. Accommodation, machines, test equipment and people are re-usable.

Reviews A review is a critical evaluation of a deliverable, business case or P3 management process.

Risk The potential of an action or event to impact on the achievement of objectives.

Risk analysis An assessment and synthesis of risk events to gain an understanding of their individual significance and their combined impact on objectives.

Risk appetite The tendency of an individual or group to take risk in a given situation.

Risk attitude The response of an individual or group to a given uncertain situation.

Risk context Describes the institutional and individual environment, attitudes and behaviours that affect the way risk arises and the way it should be managed.

Risk efficiency The principle of risk-taking to achieve the minimum level of exposure to risk for a given level of expected return.

Risk event An uncertain event or set of circumstances that would, if it occurred, have an effect on the achievement of one or more objectives.

Risk management A process that allows individual risk events and overall risk to be understood and managed proactively, optimising success by minimising threats and maximising opportunities.

Risk register A document listing identified risk events and their corresponding planned responses.

Risk response An action or set of actions to reduce the probability or impact of a threat, or to increase the probability or impact of an opportunity.

Risk techniques Used to identify, assess and plan responses to individual risks and overall risk.

Rolling wave planning The process whereby short term work is planned in detail and longer term work is planned in outline only.

Schedule A timetable showing the forecast start and finish dates for activities or events within a project, programme or portfolio.

APM Body of Knowledge 6th edition

Schedule management The process of developing, maintaining and communicating schedules for time and resource.

Scope The totality of the outputs, outcomes and benefits and the work required to produce them.

Scope management The process whereby outputs, outcomes and benefits are identified, defined and controlled.

S-curve A graphic display of cumulative costs, labour hours or other quantities, plotted against time.

Security The identification, assessment and mitigation of the risks posed to information, assets and people.

Setting The relationship of the project, programme or portfolio with its host organisation.

Share A response to an opportunity that increases its probability, impact or both by sharing the risk with a third party.

Slip chart A pictorial representation of the predicted completion dates of milestones or activities compared to their planned completion dates.

Solutions development The process of determining the best way of satisfying requirements.

Spiral life cycle A life cycle model that combines features of both iterative development and the waterfall method.

Sponsorship An important senior management role. The sponsor is accountable for ensuring that the work is governed effectively and delivers the objectives that meet identified needs.

Sprint A regular repeatable work cycle in agile development. Also known as an 'iteration'.

Stage A sub-division of the development phase of a project created to facilitate approval gates at suitable points in the life cycle.

Stakeholder The organisations or people who have an interest or role in the project, programme or portfolio, or are impacted by it.

Stakeholder management The systematic identification, analysis, planning and implementation of actions designed to engage with stakeholders.

Start-to-finish A dependency in an activity-on-node network. It indicates that one activity cannot finish until another activity has started.

Start-to-start A dependency in an activity-on-node network. It indicates that one activity cannot start until another activity has started.

Statement of work An annex to the main body of a contract that defines the detail of deliverables, timescales and management procedures.

Strategic management The identification, selection and implementation of an organisation's long term goals and objectives.

Sub-project A group of activities represented as a single activity in a higher level of the same project.

Success criteria The qualitative or quantitative measures by which the success of P3 management is judged.

Success factors and maturity
Management practices that, when
implemented, will increase the likelihood
of success of a project, programme or
portfolio. The degree to which these
practices are established and embedded
within an organisation indicates its level
of maturity.

Sunk costs Costs that are unavoidable,
even if the remaining work is terminated.

Sustainability An environmental,
social and economically integrated
approach to development that meets
present needs without compromising the
environment for future generations.

Teamwork A group of people working
in collaboration or by cooperation
towards a common goal.

Termination The decommissioning
and disposal of a deliverable at the end
of its useful life.

Threat A negative risk event; a
risk event that if it occurs will have a
detrimental effect on the objectives.

Three-point estimate An estimate
in which optimistic, most likely and
pessimistic values are given.

Timebox The production of project
deliverables in circumstances where
time and resources, including funding,
are fixed and the requirements are
prioritised and vary depending on what
can be achieved within the timebox.

Time chainage A form of graphical
schedule that shows activity in relation
to physical location as well as time.

Time-driven Control actions or
reports that are triggered by the passage
of a defined interval (e.g. monthly) are
referred to as 'time-driven'.

Time scheduling A collection of
techniques used to develop and present
schedules that show when work will be
performed.

Tolerance A permissible variation in
performance parameters.

Total float Time by which an activity
may be delayed or extended without
affecting the overall duration or violating
a target finish date.

Tranche A sub-division of the delivery
phase of a programme created to
facilitate approval gates at suitable points
in the life cycle.

Transfer A response to a threat that
reduces its probability, impact or both by
transferring the risk to a third party.

Users The group of people who are
intended to receive benefits or operate
outputs.

Value A standard, principle or quality
considered worthwhile or desirable.
In value management terms value is
defined as the ratio of 'satisfaction of
requirements' over 'use of resources'.

Value engineering Concerned with
optimising the conceptual, technical and
operational aspects of deliverables.

Value for money ratio The ratio of
monetary and non-monetary benefits
to the investment made of resources
committed.

APM Body of Knowledge 6th edition

Value management A structured approach to defining what value means to the organisation. It is a framework that allows needs, problems or opportunities to be defined and then enables review of whether these can be improved to determine the optimal approach and solution.

Value tree A graphical representation of the relationship between different factors that drive value.

V life cycle A graphical representation of a life cycle where horizontal lines connect related front and back-end phases.

Waterfall method A type of life cycle where phases are sequential.

Work package A group of related activities that are defined at the same level within a work breakdown structure.

Acronyms and abbreviations

This list of acronyms and abbreviations is made up of terms used in the sixth edition of the *APM Body of Knowledge* only. Definitions are provided where terms used are unique to the profession, or have a unique meaning in the profession.

AC	Actual cost
AIRMIC	Association of Insurance and Risk Managers
ALARP	As low as reasonably practicable
AON	Activity-on-node
APM	Association for Project Management
APMP	APM qualification at IPMA level D
ARR	Accounting rate of return
BCM	business change manager
BoK	Body of knowledge
BOOT	Build-own-operate-transfer
BSI	British Standards Institution
CAPEX	Capital expenditure
CBS	Cost breakdown structure
CMM	Capablity maturity model
CoP	Community of practice
CPA	Critical path analysis
CPD	Continuing professional development
DCF	Discounted cash flow
DSDM	Dynamic systems development method
ECHR	European Convention of Human Rights
EPMO	Enterprise project management office
EV	Earned value
EVM	Earned value management
HRM	Human resource management
IP	Intellectual property
IPMA	International Project Management Association
IRR	Internal rate of return
IS	Information systems
ISO	International Organisation for Standardisation
JCT	Joint Contracts Tribunal

JV	Joint venture
KM	Knowledge management
KPI	Key performance indicator
MoR™	Management of risk (OGC)
MSP™	Managing Successful Programmes (OGC)
MoSCoW	Must, should, could, won't
NEC	New Engineering Contract
NPV	Net present value
OBS	Organisational breakdown structure
OPEX	Operational expenditures
OPM™	Organisational Project Maturity Model
P3	Projects, programmes and portfolios
P3M3	Portfolio, Programme and Project Management Maturity Module
PBS	Product breakdown structure
PERT	Program evaluation and review technique
PESTLE	Political, economic, sociological, technical, legal, environmental
PFI	Private finance initiative
PIPMG	Pharmaceutical Industry Project Management Group
PM BoK®	A Guide to the Project Management Body of Knowledge (PMI)
PMI	Project Management Institute
PMIS	Project management information system
PMP	Project management plan
PPP	Public private partnership
PQ APM	Practioner Qualification-maps to IPMA Level C
PRAM	Project Risk Analysis and Management Guide
PRINCE2™	Projects in controlled environments
PSO	Project or programme support office
QMS	Quality management system
RACI	Responsible for action, accountable (yes/no decisions), consult before (2 way), inform after (1 way).
RAG	Red, amber, green
RAM	Responsibility assignment matrix
SIG	Specific interest group
SMART	Specific, measurable, achievable, realistic, time-framed
SoW	Statement of work
SRO	Senior responsible owner
TF	Total float
TSO	The Stationery Office
VM	Value management
WBS	Work breakdown structure

Index

APM Body of Knowledge 6th edition